Jesus
Redeemer and Divine Word

THEOLOGY AND LIFE SERIES

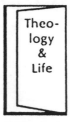

Volume 28

Jesus
Redeemer and Divine Word

by
Gerard S. Sloyan

Michael Glazier
Wilmington Delaware

ABOUT THE AUTHOR

Gerard Stephen Sloyan was ordained a priest of the diocese of Trenton in 1944. He received his S.T.L. and doctorate from the Catholic University of America, where he taught New Testament subjects for seventeen years. Since 1967 he has been Professor of Religion (New Testament) at Temple University. He is internationally respected as a theologian, biblical scholar and liturgical pioneer. Among his many publications are *The Jesus Tradition: Images of Jesus in the West* and *Catholic Morality Revisited.*

First published in 1989 by Michael Glazier, Inc., 1935 West Fourth Street, Wilmington, Delaware 19805.

Library of Congress Cataloging-in-Publication Data

Sloyan, Gerard Stephen, 1919-
   Jesus: redeemer and divine word/ by Gerard S. Sloyan,
      p. cm.—(Theology and life: vol. 28)
      ISBN 0-89453-758-X
      1. Jesus Christ—History of doctrines. 2. Salvation—History of doctrines. 3. Catholic Church—Doctrines—History. I. Title.
   II. Series: Theology and life series; v. 28.
   BT198.S585 1989
   232'.3'09—dc20   88-82456
                                           CIP

Typography by Phyllis Boyd LeVane
Printed in the United States of America

Contents

Introduction

The Christian conviction that Jesus Christ is God's chosen instrument as the savior or redeemer of the world (of the elect, a minority would say) is as widespread as commitment to the gospel. This doctrine, so central to Christianity, has never been defined as a dogma of faith, probably because it has never been seriously challenged. In the church's Scriptures the saving work of Christ is proclaimed frequently in a large variety of expressions. Christian liturgies, creeds, conciliar statements on related matters like the incarnation, and catechisms confess faith in the mystery just as unhesitatingly, but often in a much narrower range of phrases than the rich biblical possibilities held out. All Christians are able to say that Jesus saves them from their sins. Most would add, "by his sufferings and death on the cross." But not many are ready to expound their faith in this mystery lucidly to others for any protracted period. They need not do so, of course. Believers shall be saved in the measure that they respond to God's love in deed (see James 2:14-26), not in virtue of their capacity to verbalize or explain. But for Christians to give an answer for the faith that is in them is as old an injunction as the apostolic age (1 Peter 3:15). Believers and especially the educated who cannot convey to others what salvation means, who its beneficiaries are and on what terms, are in a sorry state indeed.

This inability to explain the faith one lives by is especially tragic in the late twentieth century when Christian conviction gives every appearance of dying among the thoughtful and the intellectually oriented while seeming to flourish among those who seek blessed assurance without critical inquiry. The latter

7

are only too happy to press their faith on others, often by the repetition of a dozen phrases from Scripture in a firm theological pattern (usually a radical version of Reformed faith with total biblical inerrancy appended). Others capable of a much more compelling presentation fall mute before the onslaught. Earnest proselytizers are a bore, there can be no doubt. Discreet silence is one way to attempt to silence them. Engagement often proves unsatisfactory because they prove incapable of argument in the strict sense, falling back on reiteration of their texts. But the equally earnest adherent to a more rational approach to faith is often handicapped by never having committed to memory the quite satisfactory theological formulas of a catechetical youth, or never having tried to verbalize faith convictions since arriving at maturity. It is doubtful if either response would be heard by evangelizers of a certain mindset. The more important matter is that Christians of a sound theological instinct so often find themselves disarmed by their inability to express in words the faith they hold.

This small book needs to be produced several times in each generation. It tries to tell what believers in Jesus Christ mean, or ought to mean, when they say that he is their savior (or in a Western convention of recent centuries their "personal savior"). The term "salvation" is bandied about freely in our day to describe the possession of some and the deprivation of others. The others are accused of an eternally punishable dereliction if they do not shortly avail themselves of salvation on the hawkers' terms. Whole populations are cheerfully consigned to hell by those convinced they have no part or lot in it. The young are cut off from their families, spouses from each other, and all from the crying needs of fellow humans around them, in the name of "salvation" and "reprobation" by a presumed God of boundless love. The authentic Christian teaching on God's call to reciprocate this love is an altogether richer and more comforting affair.

No attempt has been made in these pages to do original research into the historical questions presented here. There is, instead, grateful reliance on a number of collectors of patristic, medieval and modern documents of faith and historians of doctrine. The sketch could not have been written without the monumental labors of Jaroslav Pelikan in the first four volumes of his now five-volume *The Christian Tradition: A History of the Development of Doctrine.* When the church fathers or later theologians are cited, an indication is given in some cases of where an English translation may be found. When this is not done, the editorial data cited are usually enough to help a reader who takes the pains to learn whether the text exists in translation in the several extensive series of such works. Readers of Latin and Greek can normally find a citation immediately in any of the classic collections. This book is presented as a service to the less scholarly reader.

The story of the doctrine of salvation offered here is that of the Church Catholic, which makes it in the main that of Orthodoxy, the Protestant, and the Anglican traditions. Where these three and the Roman reading diverge, an honest attempt has been made to report on that fact, although the writer confesses to having given insufficient attention to the riches of the Christian East. He has tried to show those matters in the theology of salvation, or the acceptance of its benefits, in which the several Christian traditions are genuinely at odds and those many more where their differences are of emphasis rather than essence.

A word of gratitude must be recorded to Ms. Nadia Kravchenko, who has learned to her rue that *manu*script means precisely that, and to Joseph A. Quinn, the vigilant editor of this manuscript. Finally, to Mr. Michael Glazier, the publisher, who brings books to birth maieutically in the older manner of publishers.

1

Who Do People Say I Am?

Anyone who reads the gospels with care comes to realize that they are not only centered on the life and teaching of Jesus but are more concerned with what he accomplished than with who he was. There is, of course, a concern with his identity. It takes the form of situating him less in his own time and place than in relation to his people, Israel, over the ages, and to the God of Israel. The gospel indications of who Jesus is are expressed in the titles that describe him: "son of Mary" (Mark 6:3), "son of Joseph" (John 1:45), a Nazarene (Mark 1:24), "a Galilean" (Matthew 26:69), but also "Son of man" (Matthew 8:20; 24:30), "Son of God" (Matthew 14:33), "the Son" (Mark 13:32; John 14:13), "the Word of God become human" (John 1:14), "the Messiah or Christ" (v. 41), "he who is to come" (Matthew 11:3), "a Savior" (Luke 2:11), "the achiever of eternal redemption" (Hebrews 9:12) and "the Lord" (Acts 1:21). There are other titles by which Jesus is designated outside the gospels. Some of them are "King of kings and Lord of lords" (Revelation 19:16), "the living one" (1:18), "the Alpha and the Omega" (22:13), and "an advocate with the Father" (1 John 2:1).

The list is far from complete. If it were to be completed the net effect would be much the same. Jesus was a Jew of a recognizable tribe, family and place. He was someone who, at the same time, stood in a unique relation to God. He had suprahuman, perhaps even fully divine, status. He was called by God to do a work in the service of all humanity. That work can be called global or cosmic. All things came to be through him (John 1:3; Hebrews 1:2). He rules over all creatures, including the angels (Hebrews 1:6). He has radically improved the condition of all creation before God, and the end of what he will achieve for those who believe in him is nowhere in sight (1 John 3:2). Thus do the writers of the apostolic era describe the man and his work.

The claims made for Jesus are such that both he and those who wrote him up in the twenty-seven canonical books (the "New Testament"; see 2 Corinthians 3:6; Luke 22:20 for clues to that description of the literature of an event) have been accused many times of self-delusion or grandiosity. A few years ago a book appeared which had as its sub-title, *How the Kingdom of God Became the Church*. Almost needless to add, the third of three chapters was entitled, "How Jesus Became God." Ever since a pagan philosopher named Celsus wrote the first such book we know of (ca. 180) someone has been explaining how the beliefs people have about Jesus came to be. A more careful reading of the early Christian writings than pagans or ex-Christians normally give them provides the answer. For the latter, things began with the usual, the ordinary, the explainable which, after a certain period of time, became the unusual, the mysterious, the uniquely unexplainable. The trouble with all such tidy theories of evolution is that Jesus gets in their way. Fragmentary though our historical knowledge of him is and satisfactory as our knowledge of the "history of religions" to account for him seems to be, there he stands—so to say in the middle of the road. He exacts faith in himself despite all the best efforts of apologists and skeptics.

A poet once wrote of a much lesser figure: "Others abide our question. Thou art free." The man of Nazareth seems to have been acknowledged as divine and the Church as prelude to the kingdom without a great deal of help from his friends. In a hoary anecdote, Napoleon reportedly said to his captive of five years, Pope Pius VII: "I will destroy that Church of yours!" The pope is supposed to have replied: "I doubt it. We priests, after all, have not succeeded in eighteen hundred years." Jesus abides all questions and remains free of the restraints his friends and foes alike put on him (see John 7:45-49). Meantime, millions continue to look to him as their prime advocate with God and the savior of the world.

Some Early Christological Challenges and Responses

The paradox of the opening lines of this chapter should not elude us. While the earliest Christian writings were most concerned to underscore *what Jesus accomplished*—referred to variously as "redemption," "salvation," "reconciliation," "atonement," new "life" for the world—the first among believers in him to sing outside the choir had the problem of *who he was*. This requires a brief look at the Church's early christology, a subject with which this book will be only peripherally concerned. It was variously denied by some of those who professed faith in him that he could have saved anyone if he could not save himself from death (the scandal of a suffering or "passible" redeemer, as they referred to him); that he could be anything but a creature, since as son he was "begotten of God"; that he could be divine and human without being son of Mary as distinct from Son of God; and that his full possession of godhead was compatible with a complete humanity, for why claim a human soul for him if the word who was with God rendered it needless?

The first of these denials constituted the gnostic and docetic threats—the teaching of second- and third-century Christians who believed, in one sense, too much about him but in another, too little. If he was divine he could not be human. If he was spirit he could not be body. These views of Jesus first peaked, then subsided, without the need for settlement at a churchwide council. But they lingered on as suspicions of any limitation about him, anything finite or material in him. In a word, early Christian gnostics thought that his taking flesh was so crude a concept that it could only have happened in appearance. And they awaited their day.

The second denial concerned Jesus' status as God because sole-begotten of God. It was met with a counter-affirmation at the Council of Nicaea in 325, which the emperor Constantine summoned. Nicaea is in modern mainland Turkey, across the

Bosporus from Istanbul and somewhat south. The decision of the assembled bishops there was not without its political overtones but it did reflect the majority view. This view was by no means the unanimous one, as the event proved. The council rejected as "blasphemous" the teaching of Arius of Alexandria "which affirmed that 'the Son of God is from what is not' and 'there was a when-he-was-not,' saying also that the Son of God, in virtue of his free-will, is capable of evil and good, and calling him a creature and a work."[1] Thus does the historian Socrates transmit the letter of the synod of Nicaea condemning Arius. Its creed (not to be confused with the familiar creed from the Sunday liturgy, read and approved at Chalcedon in 451) ran as follows:

> And in the Lord Jesus Christ, the Son of God, *begotten of the Father*, only begotten, *that is, of the substance of the Father*, God of God, Light of Light, *true God of true God, begotten not made, of one substance with the Father*, through whom all things were made, *things in heaven and things on the earth*; who for us humans and for our salvation *came down* and was made flesh, *and became man*, suffered, and rose on the third day, ascended into the heavens, is coming to judge living and dead.[2]

The underscored phrases were additions by the council fathers to the creed of Caesarea in Palestine which its Arian-sympathizing bishop Eusebius had proposed for discussion. Remove them and you can see what Arius and his followers were able to chant liturgically in good conscience. Jesus Christ was "the Son of God" and even "God" for them, the one "through whom all things were made." But these were ways of describing the "first born of all creation," a God-like creature who shared in the work of the divine but was not "true God of true God." In Arian eyes the uniqueness of the divine origina-

---

[1] Henry Bettenson, ed., *Documents of the Christian Church*, 2d ed.; (London: Oxford University Press, 1963), pp. 57-58.

[2] *Ibid.,* p. 35 (adapted).

tion of all (*monarchia*) made it impossible for anyone "begotten of God," even the "only Son" of the New Testament (John 1:14, 18; 3:16, 18) to be ultimately anything but a creature. Continuing the review of challenges to the Church's faith in who Jesus is—a New Testament faith expressed in prayers which the people prayed publicly every Sunday—we come to the fear of some fourth-century theologians in Syrian Antioch that belief in his full humanity was threatened by the way belief in his divinity was being expressed. Despite the creedal phrases that this "God from God" "became man" and "suffered," the Alexandrian spirit in theology was such that it shrank from any talk of "two natures" in Christ as a threat to his unity. To describe things this way is to suggest that the theological vocabulary was already in place. It was not, since it was to be hammered out only in the first half of the fifth century by men like the chief Alexandrian litigant St. Cyril, bishop of that city (d. 444), and the chief Antiochean representative, Theodore of Mopsuestia (d. 428). The Egyptian ("Coptic") and the Syrian outlooks on everything were at stake here, even though the two peoples, both Semitic, had adopted the Hellenic tongue and philosophic mode of argument.

A pupil of Theodore, Nestorius who was bishop of Constantinople (428-31), thought that the union of divine and human in Christ was not well attested to by the title of "Godbearer" (*theotokos* that was being given to Mary, common since Origen's day (d. ca. 254). "Christ-bearer" (*christotokos*), he thought, conveyed the reality of the incarnation better, since to say "Christ" was to say both God and man. He maintained that the divine Word and the son of Mary were undivided in the "*prosōpon* (person) of the union," a new and mysterious unity wrought by divine power. His antagonist Cyril, hearing the stress on duality, interpreted this as an "indwelling Logos" in the man Jesus. He secured Nestorius' condemnation, first at a synod of Rome (430) and then at the council of Ephesus (431). Nestorius was excommunicated in 432 at a Roman synod with the concurrence of Pope Celestine. The council's adverse judgment was in the form of twelve "anathemas" (condemned propositions) framed by Cyril against Nestorius, and the second of two dogmatic letters addressed to him by Cyril. This identified Nestorianism as a heresy, whether the man whose name it bore held it or not. Constituting the heretical view, according to Cyril as adopted by the Council, would be "dividing the persons (*hypostaseis*) after their union," "distributing between two characters or persons the expressions used about Christ in the gospels . . . applying some to the man, conceived of separately, apart from the Word . . . others exclusively to the Word," and "calling Christ 'a God-bearing man.'"[3] Despite Nestorius' attempts to keep the human Jesus from being submerged in the union with deity, Nestorius' name will forever be connected with the error of seeing in Jesus a divine person and a human person in a "moral," not a "substantial" union. The Cyrillian phrase for such a real union was "hypostatic" (*kath'hypostasin*), meaning in a single person.

St. Cyril died in 444, not before receding from some of his more extreme positions which led logically to the heresy of Eutyches. The two decades after Ephesus were marked by dissatisfaction with its settlement in both camps and a great deal of imperial-ecclesiastical politics besides. Both Alexandrians and Antiocheans maintained that Ephesus had departed from the truth of Nicaea, even though the Cyrillians seemed to have much the better of it.

A synod was held in Constantinople in 448 charging the aged archimandrite of a monastery there, Eutyches, with heresy. He said in response to the archbishop of Constantinople, Flavian: "I confess that before the union our Lord had two natures, but after the union I confess one single nature."[4] This position that there is one nature in Christ is called "monophysitism" and is irreversibly connected with the name of Eutyches. He was condemned by the synod and appealed to Leo, bishop of Rome, who upheld Flavian. Eutyches had "never said that the body of our Lord and God was *homoousios* (of the same

---

[3] *Ibid.*, pp. 65-68.

[4] Jaroslav Pelikan, *The Christian Tradition. A History of the Development of Doctrine 1. The Emergence of the Catholic Tradition (100-600)* (Chicago: University of Chicago Press, 1971, p. 262), quoting *Acta Conciliorum Oecumenicorum*, 2-1-1:143. Strasburg, 1914.

substance) with us,"[5] it is reported, "...but I will use [the term] now, since your Holiness demands it."[6] The fear of attributing to Christ a limited humanity like ours in its sinfulness, after its union with divinity, is evident. Eutyches gave as his reason that this might deny Christ's being the Son of God. He claimed "the blessed Cyril" as the one from whom he learned to hold for a single nature after the union.

The condemnation of Eutyches did not sit well with the emperor Theodosius II, who in the next year (449) convened a council at Ephesus under the presidency of Cyril's successor in Alexandria, Dioscoros. At it, Eutyches was restored and Flavian deposed, as part of the anathema declared on anyone who taught two natures.[7] Pope Leo I was later to tag this political *coup* a "*latrocinium*" or robber synod (Letter 45). The emperor's death intervened in 450. One year later a council was held at Chalcedon across the straits from Constantinople, reinstating the Flavian condemnation of Eutyches.

The chief architect of the Chalcedonian settlement was the bishop of Rome, Leo I (440-61), who wrote a letter to the eastern patriarch Flavian in 449 on the question of the precise union of Christ's two natures. St. Augustine, dead nearly twenty years, was the chief influence on him in these matters. Leo was doubtless also familiar with John Cassian's treatise against Nestorius and the writings of Prosper of Aquitaine and Gaudentius of Brescia (Leo knew no Greek). Surprisingly, the more than 500, mostly eastern bishops who assembled at Chalcedon invested the Latin document with supreme authority, giving Rome for the first time "a determining role in the definition of Christian dogma."[8] Leo's *Tomus* (booklet) may have won acceptance for its straightforwardness and clarity, avoiding the subtleties which kept the "two-natures" and "one-nature" parties apart. At the same time, its compromising

---

[5] *Ibid.*, p. 271, quoting Conc. Chal. *Acta* (Mansi 6:741f.)

[6] Bettenson, p. 69, quoting Mansi, p. 744 [741, 745].

[7] Pelikan, p. 263, quoting *ACO*, 2-I-1:140.

[8] Judith Herrin, *The Formation of Christendom* (Princeton: Princeton University Press, 1987), p. 103.

avoidance of their positions resulted in Chalcedon's being the church's "last word on the subject," as it is sometimes called, in only a limited sense. The subsequent councils of II Constantinople (553) and III Constantinople (681) were, respectively, a Cyrillian repudiation of anything smacking of the clear Antiochean distinction between the two natures (which Pope Vigilius seems to have signed under duress) and a denial of the monothelete heresy, a corollary of monophysitism which held that there was but one will in Christ. The theologically innocent Pope Honorius accepted the monothelete teaching, joining Sergios, patriarch of Constantinople, in a bid to win back the monophysites to Chalcedonian unity.

The agreement arrived at in 451 has to be recognized as a fragile one. Its careful balance between the two natures in Christ in a single person has been threatened from then until now by a tendency toward the monophysite position—an easy transition from the one person who is divine to a human nature that merely clothes this person. That view of Jesus Christ is formally heretical but it is widely held. Here is the heart of the definition approved at Chalcedon. The translation is Bettenson's (p. 73), adapted:

> Therefore, following the holy Fathers, we all with one accord teach people to acknowledge one and the same Son, our Lord Jesus Christ, at once complete in divinity and complete in humanity, truly God and truly man, consisting also of a rational soul and a body; of one substance (*homoousios*) with the Father as regards his divinity, and at the same time of one substance with us as regards his humanity; like us in all respects apart from sin; as regards his divinity, begotten of the Father before all ages, yet as regards his humanity begotten, for us and for our salvation, of the Virgin Mary, the God-bearer (*theotokos*; Lat., *deipara*); one and the same Christ, Son, Lord, Only-begotten, recognized in two natures (*physesin*), without confusion (*asyngchytōs*), without change (*atreptōs*), without division (*adiairetōs*), without separation (*achoristōs*); the distinction of natures being in no way annulled by the union, but rather the characteristics of each nature being preserved and coming together to form one person (*prosōpon*) and

one subsistence (*hypostasis*), not as parted or separated into two persons, but one and the same Son and Only-begotten God the Word, Lord Jesus Christ; even as the prophets from earliest times spoke of him, and our Lord Jesus Christ himself taught us, and the creed of the Fathers has handed down to us.

What the Christological Definitions Meant to Do

The focus of this book will be on the phrase "for us and for our salvation," which was not the primary focus of the definition. That, the framers took for granted. What was of central concern? The way in which the manhood or humanness of Jesus Christ was united—conjoined—to the godhead of the eternal Word was the point at issue. Even though both sides in the dispute ("all sides" would describe it better) maintained that the exact nature of the union was an impenetrable mystery, they often wrote and acted as if it were available to them. The formula adopted, like all doctrinal definitions, could hope only to deny what had been alleged falsely in the matter, not to affirm what was true. To do the latter inevitably gives the impression that the affirmations made encompass the mysterious, revealed truth, Thus, even the statement that "God is" can be deceptive if it leads the hearer to assume that the speaker has an adequate knowledge of what is meant by "God." To say that there is God requires immediate declarations of all that is unknown about God. To call God infinite or timeless is close to the mark because it denies to God categories of which we humans have some experience, namely the limited character of space and time, without presuming to say what the limitlessness consists in.

All the litigants in the fifth-century christological debates were well aware of these limitations of speech. Yet they did not succeed very well in keeping a guard on the prose of their debates. They gave the impression by the use of the words for divinity (or godhead) and humanity (or manhood) that they were discussing two realities, both in the same order, which they understood. Of course they were doing no such thing; not two realities in the same order of magnitude—a conclusion that no one would draw—but two realities in the same order of being, which the unsophisticated might easily conclude. God and the human creature are so infinitely unlike that the mystery is that they can be spoken of as one person (meaning subsistent entity) at all. Jews and Muslims agree that it is unthinkable; Hindus and Buddhists would not have quite the same problem if they were faced with it. The point at issue is that "divinity" and "humanity," when constantly coupled in theological discourse, lull the user into supposing that two comparable elements are at issue like hydrogen and oxygen, or the musician and the physicist, in the same person. Nothing could be further from the truth. God cannot "figure as one factor among others in some sort of natural relationship."[9]

Alerted to the perils of this mode of discourse, the bishops at Chalcedon made the heart of their definition four denials, not four affirmations, about the incarnation, hoping in that way to point to revealed truth by identifying the erroneous opposites to it. At this date it is not easy to identify who held the four distinct positions reprobated; some are easier to deduce than others. But clearly the two "natures" (*physeis*) of the "one and the same Christ"—whatever deity may mean from a human perspective—are not confused (making a new divine-human substance), not changed (becoming more, less, or other than each had been), not divided (into two subsistences or persons), and not separated (into two sets of characteristics proper to each nature but not to the person).

It is sometimes asserted that this conciliar definition resorted to philosophical language because the speech of the Bible and the liturgy, being pictographic, was unable to convey the church's faith beyond the possibility of being misconstrued. That is not quite what happened. The various positions in the christological debate were argued metaphysically in treatises of varying length and subtlety. No one thought that the resort from one symbol system ("language game") to another removed the mystery, only that it could convey what the Bible taught with less possibility of heretical denial. When some

[9]Richard A. Norris, *Understanding the Faith of the Church* (New York: Seabury, 1979), p. 166.

proclaimed as the Church's faith what the Bible did not teach they could be shown up by having their teaching transposed into other words that said what the Bible did teach. Those who came to Chalcdeon—some more than others—knew the arguments of the years since Nicaea. They did not frame a new argument. They adopted a powerful rhetorical instrument in the language of the familiar arguments. When it came to calling Jesus Christ the one who he is, they opted for one "person and subsistence," knowing that different parties attached different meanings to the terms. One "person *or* subsistence" might have been taken for a declaration that the two terms meant the same. This the fathers knew was denied in various quarters. Their phrase "one person *and* subsistence" was a way of saying, "whatever 'oneness' may mean to you." As to duality, the phrase "in two natures" granted to the Antiocheans more than the Alexandrians wished. Cyril's third anathema of Nestorius, adopted at Ephesus, spoke of a "combination according to a union of natures" (*"kata henōsin physikēn,"* more accurately nature-union), with "union" the operative word. Like all compromises, the definition gave something to everyone and denied something to everyone. The one-person-one-nature people derived least comfort from it and resisted it longest.

Richard Norris, suspecting that the philosophical niceties of the several debates going on in that century will escape most moderns, has caught the thrust of the definition neatly. He says that Chalcedon's assertion about Jesus Christ is fourfold:

> That everything which Jesus was and did has a single ultimate source—God in his Word. Jesus' person and his career are ways in which the Word or Son of God is actively present in human affairs ... Jesus ... in the last resort ... is the Word of God....
>
> That everything which Jesus was and did is a genuine human reality ... one not only can but must talk about Jesus as one would about any other human being. The Incarnation is not an abolition but an affirmation of creaturely human existence....
>
> That these two ways of talking about Jesus really are

> *different* ways of talking. . . . Each . . . sets him, as it were
> in a different framework of understanding. The "natures"
> are genuinely distinct.
>
> Finally . . . that both of these ways of talking—that which
> refers everything about Jesus to the Word of God, and . . .
> sees everything about him as an authentic human reality—
> belong together. . . . In him, the divine and the human
> coincide.[10]

The last few pages summarize a phase of Church history it is
doubtful we can understand. There was an immense gap, a
chasm, in the popular mind of those days between deity and
humanity. When we today think about godhead at all it tends
to be in terms of the things which God can do and the human
race cannot do yet. Angels seldom figure in our thoughts;
hence the notion of a supreme angelic creature called "Word"
through whom God created all that is exceeds our powers of
conception. Such would simply never occur to us. Our brains,
moreover, have been so addled by a science fiction that is
more fiction than science that when we think of a person of
superhuman stature or capabilities we can only think of a
transfer of parts. Only a cerebral transplant or some other
improbable surgery—sometimes it is the ingestion of unex-
plained potions—can account for a person's going from
normal human limits to few limits or none. For us, some
quantitative addition of what had not previously been there is
required.

Christians of the fourth- and fifth-century Hellenist world
operated with entirely different categories than ours. Spirit
represented perfection, the body imperfection. The call of Jesus
to be "perfect as your heavenly Father is perfect" had come to
mean setting limits aside—achieving that state in which one no
longer suffers. The chief benefit Jesus had won for humanity
was immortality: not precisely an incorporeal existence in the
future but one marked by neither alteration nor change. Jesus'
experience of suffering—even simple things like hunger, thirst

[10] *Ibid.*, p. 168.

and fatigue—was not a consolation but a stumbling-block. His undergoing a shameful death in a helpless condition was the supreme scandal. To underscore that Jesus had exclusively the nature of a creature, Arius stressed all the passages in the New Testament that bespoke human limits. He attributed the gospel deeds of power to Jesus' role as agent of the divine. The patristic world celebrated sacraments as signs of salvation but paradoxically resisted matter as the fitting partner of spirit, the divine Spirit above all. The Word had become flesh but in doing so proved to some that it was a creaturely utterance of God. For others among the anti-Arians who knew the Word to be true God of true God, godhead must somehow have absorbed this manhood and transformed it utterly. It was either united with it in a way that deprived it of limitation or created an amalgam in which the divine eliminated the distinctively human.

In certain respects the ancient world of heresy resembled the modern. The deity within manipulated the humanity without. God's glorious puppet was *essentially* the immortal Word somehow enfleshed, not a full and complete human being mysteriously joined in a single person to the divine Logos. The definition of Chalcedon declared him to be such but the Catholic centuries heard "consubstantial with the Father" more clearly than "human being."

Because our starting point is not that of the people of that age, we have trouble grasping the appeal the positions above described had for them. Modern evangelicals who have little use for post-biblical tradition cleave to the faith of Nicaea and Chalcedon without having heard of those debates, supposing that the New Testament delivers that faith full-blown to anyone who reads it attentively. Catholics have heard of the councils vaguely but do not know their import except as victories over heresies they once had to memorize. Both hear the gospels and epistles expounded on Sundays in a way that leaves them wondering what the problem is. Jesus was conceived miraculously, had the gift of reading hearts and foretelling the future, did things that only God could do such as raising the dead and himself rising from the dead, and sent down the Spirit on the Church after his return to the Father. It is quite true that he reacted with human impatience to his disciples' dullness of heart, described himself as a vagrant who had no place to lay his head, and endured an agony of both dread and incredible torture before being executed as an enemy of the Roman state. The net effect of all this on most hearers (and even careful readers) of the New Testament is that Jesus was "God" without further nuance, someone who foresaw all that would happen in his passion and steeled himself to endure the excruciating pain of a few hours for our sakes, secure in the knowledge that within days he would emerge glorious from the tomb.

The "popular monophysitism" which is the faith of most Christians does not prepare them for the jolt they receive on first discovering that Jesus really was human as the creeds insist, with all the limits that this entails. Sometimes it is an academic course in the gospels or a book about them that brings this home. A serious reading of the New Testament can have the same effect. It is now thirty years since John A.T. Robinson, the Anglican bishop of Woolwich (near Southwark on the Thames) wrote a short book for which his wife proposed the title, *Honest to God.* The book sold 350,000 copies in its first seven months in 1963 and translations were shortly prepared into seven languages. It was largely warmed-over Bonhoeffer, Bultmann and Tillich but with none of their Germanic heaviness. Robinson confronted an unchurched English population with the comforting myths with which it had dwelt at ease and demonstrated their untenable character in that form. He then proposed the sublime *mythos* which is the vehicle of an unsettling New Testament faith in God. This apologist for the gospel at full strength and in recognizable language found himself receiving up to 4,000 letters a day from around the world: some in gratitude, others making further inquiry, but many pillorying him for his "faithlessness." He robbed many of the stone of a false faith and offered the bread of a true one. The offer was appreciated by many but unpalatable to many more.

Jesus as Son of God and Word Enfleshed: The Gospels

The readers of this book are invited to go on a tour of *soteriology*—the theology of Jesus' work as savior—with a basis of *christology*—Jesus as the Christ of God—laid in this early chapter. The New Testament authors did not go about things in any such methodical way. They presented him as someone already believed in, as a man sent from God who was with God from the beginning, who had as his work to do the salvation of the world. The formulas recited in our liturgies are authentic expressions of that faith. The gospels read out in their current lectionary form present Jesus in all his mysterious paradox, yet a smooth and unquestioned portrait of him as the figure of church dogma may be the only one that is heard. Jesus is someone who has to be lived up to in the struggle called life. Some readers of these lines may have heard the challenge only lately, others not yet. He is a redeemer only for those who have experienced the need of redemption. With life a chaos to which faith in Christ has restored some semblance of order, the rhetoric of salvation makes some sense. Otherwise, it is just parroted words.

The four evangelists wrote for people who already believed in him in their Hellenized Jewish way. They were not medieval Europeans, industrialized North Americans or emerging Third World people from much older cultures than their own. The thoroughgoing Semites who knew some Greek must have found passages in the gospels hard to understand, the Graeco-Roman pagans the same. That is because these writings drew on the worlds of both and were not quite at home in either. The thought world of Jesus and his followers was that of apocalyptic Judaism, an anxious waiting for God to break in on Israel's history and usher in "the final days." This expectation may have been even more heightened in the days in which his followers produced their four documents of faith in him than in his brief career. It would not be long after the destruction of Jerusalem by the Romans in 70 of the Common Era that an earnest corps of rabbis would begin to try to talk the Jews out of these dreams of the future, dreams that were the matrix from which the Christian movement was born. If that revisionist spirit was already launched in Palestine the gospels do not reflect it. They present a man who, because God has already raised him up from the dead, will come in glory "with clouds" at the end and be disclosed to all as Messiah. It was hard for the gospel writers to report on Jesus' activity in

Palestine without being influenced by their knowledge that he was the risen one. They tried but the attempt was not entirely successful. The teaching they relayed as having come from his lips was that of a youthful sage who spoke the wisdom of God. It would be centuries before most of the nuggets of wisdom and the stories he shared would turn up in rabbinic literature. Some were quite unique to him. His teaching centered, not on himself, but on God's rule over an obedient Israel. He envisioned this, like any Jew, as a matter of God's mysterious future but also as something that impended. All the evidence points to his having thought its onset was near and that he had a call from God not simply to preach it but to bring it on in his own person. The one thing about Jesus the gospels are clearest on is the greatness of his conception of God and the nearness to God he exuded. Those who heard him seem to have been convinced that God had spoken a word in their hearing.

The gospel record of Jesus as an exorcist and healer, even as a resuscitator of the dead and master of nature, is such that he cannot not have been a wonder-worker. There was surely elaboration in the accounts we have, not least to bring his deeds into line with those of Moses, Elijah and other great ones from the past. But it is unthinkable, on grounds of critical history alone, that his only power was that of the spoken word. Through him, God did more. Tales of healing and multiplying food attach only to those who, in fact, heal and feed miraculously. It is impossible to get the rumor started any other way. Jesus became "the Lord" and "the Christ" retrospectively to those sources the evangelists drew upon. The latter title was so commonly attributed to him over decades that it became as if his proper name in one proverbial utterance: a believer was someone who was "Christ's" (Mark 9:41). Whether Jesus spoke of himself customarily as "the son of man," as the first three gospels have it, is much debated. It was probably a designation of the early church for him derived from various apocalyptic writings. The evangelists used this third-person reference to himself to describe him as *the man* but also as the sufferer and the coming glorious one. This was the paradox that believers in him could not get over: he who was uniquely "son of God" was all of these.

The impression Jesus made on any who knew him was memorable. It was not simply the crowds he drew. It was the recollections he inspired. These caused witness upon witness after he was glorified to say, "It was this way," and "No, it was that way," with all the conflicting testimony that attends a figure too large for words to contain.

There are still many other things that Jesus did, yet if they were written about in detail, I doubt there would be room enough in the entire world to hold the books to record them (John 21:25).

What there *was* room for was a great many written collections of what he said and what he did. The former were made up of his brief, pithy sayings and his short, short stories. These were assembled as if he had given them as discourses on individual occasions. There were, of course, occasions, hundreds of them, but in the telling his words came to be associated with his deeds of power. Conversely, accounts of his deeds culminated in his words. At a certain point the first of four authors—the man we know as Mark—wove together from the rich collection of preaching turned writing that was available to him a narrative of the type we call "gospel." He began it with the preaching of reform by a certain John from whom Jesus accepted a river bath in the Jordan and capped it with an account of Jesus' last hours of humiliation, then glory. Two other early writers give every evidence of having Mark's gospel handy and making copious use of it: Matthew who used 600 of Mark's 661 verses (as they later came to be divided) and who often altered Mark's meaning with his new contexts; and Luke who used Mark less but changed him more. These two had access to a collection of Jesus' sayings that Mark did not, more than fifty of which they employed. They also brought Jesus' origins back beyond his adult baptism to conception in his mother's womb. One was quite clear, the other less so, that Jesus had God as his father in a way that Joseph, his mother's husband-to-be, was not. A fourth writer, John, possessed many of the same reminiscences as the other three but invariably used them differently. It is conventional to say that John was the last of the four to write but there are few solid grounds for

maintaining this. "After Mark" is the safer thing to say, just as
with the other two. Mark set the tone by devising the literary
genre known as gospel.
All four are marked by a consistency in their portrayal of
Jesus. This is true even though John has him speak in rolling
periodic sentences and not the swift, sharp verbal strokes that
characterize him in the other three. John's Jesus consistently
expresses the Johannine community's faith in him. That is
likewise true of Mark, Matthew and Luke, but not in so
marked a degree. For all four Jesus is a completely human
figure who is not introspective but is supremely knowledgeable.
He knows the future, reads human hearts—in John more than
the others—communicates constantly with the God he calls
"my Father," and does all in his power to press home the
seriousness of accepting God's rule (kingdom, reign) as life's
sole great prize. There is one saying of Jesus reported by Mark
in 13:32 which Matthew quotes unchanged in 24:36. That is
unusual because Matthew normally shies away from any
limitations which Mark attributes to Jesus. It is this: "As to
the exact day or hour, no one knows it, neither the angels in
heaven, nor the Son, but the Father only." It would seem to be
authentic precisely because it puts limits to Jesus' knowledge.
The divinizing process would ordinarily have rejected it had he
not said it. At the same time, Matthew's gospel contains what
has been called a synoptic thunderbolt in a Johannine sky:
"Everything has been given over to me by my Father. No one
knows the Son but the Father, and no one knows the Father
but the Son—and anyone to whom the Son wishes to reveal
him" (Matthew 11:27; cf. John 10:14-15; 17:25). The only acceptable explanation is a strong recollection, wherever the
story of Jesus was told, that he enjoyed an intimacy with God
that was greater than that of Moses or any prophet, a knowledge of God that by any standard must be termed suprahuman.
    John's gospel is the chief repository among the four of a
christology like Chalcedon's that weds his call to messiahship
(4:26) and capacity for suffering and death (19:16-42) to his
preexistence as a Word of God (1:1) in the inmost recesses of
godhead (*eis ton kolpon* 1:18): "and what God was, the Word
was" (*kai theos ēn ho logos*, 1:1). Jesus in John, speaking in
the phrasing of the "the first Christian believer," says: "Before

Abraham came to be, I AM" (8:58); "The Father and I are one" (10:30); "All that the Father has belongs to me" (16:15); "I will send the Counselor, the Spirit of truth from the Father" (15:26); but also, "The Father is greater than I" (14:28), underscoring the clear distinction between God and God's Word who in this gospel becomes flesh (1:18). The Father loves Jesus on this account, that he lays down his life that he may take it up again (10:17); but he cries out "I thirst" to fulfill the Scripture (19:28) and dies (19:30, 33) and is buried (v. 42) nonetheless. The Johannine church like the other three records its awe in the face of this person, of whose "unity" none has any doubt. This awe takes the form of a suspicion that he may be more than human before his glorification. It rises to the conviction afterward that he participates in godhead, coloring the total gospel report (see John 20:9).[11]

Jesus as Son of God and Lord: The Pauline Corpus and Beyond

Elsewhere in the New Testament there are seven authentic letters of Paul, all written in the '50s, which testify to his faith in who Jesus is, although he is primarily interested in what he achieved. In one place Paul speaks of Jesus' status as a human being and a Jew "under the law" as part of his declaration that deliverance from the law will be succeeded by adoption (*huiothesia*) as a result of God's sending God's (*autou*) son (Galatians 4:4-5). In another seeming quotation from a creed, Paul speaks of Jesus' Davidic descent (Romans 1:3); he is "one man" (5:12, 15) in contrast to another, Adam. Paul refers to the cross so frequently that there can be no doubt he knows Jesus died that way. The total silence of the apostle on Jesus' earthly career, for whatever reason, is well known, as is his exclusive concentration on the paschal three days (e.g., "died ... was buried ... and rose," 1 Corinthians 15:3-4; cf.

---

[11] For "Jesus' Sense of Sonship," see James D.G. Dunn, *Christology in the Making. A New Testament Inquiry into the Origins of the Doctrine of the Incarnation* (Philadelphia: Westminster, 1980), pp. 22-33, summarizing his earlier *Jesus and the First Christians as Reflected in the New Testament* (London: SCM, 1975).

Romans 1:4; for "his blood," see 3:25). Paul speaks of Jesus as "God's Son" 17 times and "Lord" nearly 230 times. Notable references to Jesus' sonship of God occur in Romans 5:10; 8:32; and Galatians 2:20. While the pre-Pauline formula that underlies Romans 1:2-4 indicates that Jesus' divine sonship stemmed from his resurrection, there is no doubt that elsewhere Paul speaks of Jesus as God's son prior to his resurrection and exaltation. There was simply no Jewish concept of incarnation as Paul wrote, and it is entirely unlikely he was introducing it in Galatians 4:4-5. The same is true of Romans 8:3 ("God, by sending his son in the likeness of sinful flesh") where again, as the text proceeds, the thrust is soteriological, not incarnational. Just as in 1:3-4, however, Paul is affirming Jesus' sonship of God throughout his entire life and not just as a result of the culminating drama. For Paul, his christology *is* his soteriology: Jesus could accomplish what he did for humanity only because he is God's son. Arguing Paul's belief in Jesus' preexistence from Galatians 4:4-5 and Romans 8:3 looks easy but proves hard. Finally, Romans 9:5, in context, does not seem to express belief in Christ as preexistent God because it is best punctuated: "And from them came the Christ as to his human origins." Period. Then, without the doubtful textual addition, "being": "God who is over all be blessed forever. Amen." St. Paul thinks of Jesus' sonship of God as a lifelong condition, a small but important advance on the previous apologetic use of Psalm 2:7 in which Jesus "became" son of God upon his resurrection.

The pastoral letters 1 and 2 Timothy and Titus and the catholic epistle James do not have anything to say about Jesus as son of God. They call him "Lord," "Christ," the one mediator between God and humanity (see 1 Timothy 2:5), someone with whom those who persevere will reign (2 Timothy 2:12), the final judge (4:8) and the savior (Titus 2:14; 3:6). In 1 Peter, God is "the Father of our Lord Jesus Christ" (1:3). The so-called "epistle" to the Hebrews *seems* to be the first New Testament writing to embrace the thought of a preexistent divine sonship (1:1-14; 4:14) but it may be more of an idea and a purpose in the mind of God, in the author's Platonic idealism, than personal divine being in the John mold. When Revelation praises Jesus Christ (the latter title already part of his name, 1:1, 2, 5), it does so as "the ruler of kings on earth" (1:5), "one like a son of man" (1:13), "the Son of God" (2:18), "the Lion of the tribe of Judah, the Root of David" (5:5), " a Lamb as if slain" (5:6), "the Word of God" (19:13), "King of kings and Lord of lords" (v. 16), "the Alpha and the Omega, the first and the last, the beginning and the end" (22:13), and "the bright morning star" (v. 16).

The Witness of the Second Century to Who Jesus Is

It is an unfair complaint against first-century Christianity to find there a Jesus who is indisputably Lord of the end-time in present and future glory and not someone who makes the phrases of the creed of Nicaea spring immediately to the lips. A certain sympathy must be shown for devout village agnostics—and Jehovah's Witnesses—who pound their Bibles and ask to be shown the page on which it says that Jesus Christ is God. St. Paul's constant coupling of God and Christ in his basic "binitarianism" will not satisfy them, nor his trinitarianism in 1 Thessalonians 1:2-5 or 2 Corinthians 13:14. The Matthean baptismal formula (28:19) will not do it. Neither will the statement of Colossians that in Christ "all the fullness of godhead dwells bodily" (2:9). The Arians knew these texts in their native Greek and went unmoved. Bringing to the attention of modern challengers the shipboard letters of Ignatius of Antioch (d. ca. 110, probably before some New Testament material was written) will prove quite useless, given their commitment to the canon finalized in the late fourth century as the only dependable witness to early belief. But for those who know the early testimonies to Christian faith to be a continuum, the exercise can be extremely helpful.

It should be recalled that Antioch on the Orontes (modern southeastern Turkey), where this "bishop from Syria" as Ignatius called himself (Romans 2.2) hailed from, was the city from the ambit of which Matthew's gospel probably originated—some would even say all four gospels. The gospels were fifty years old or less at the time Ignatius wrote his six letters to the Province of Asia's churches and one to Polycarp in Smyrna, on his way to martyrdom in Rome. In them, he calls Jesus Christ "our Savior" (Ephesians 1.1) and "God's son" (4.2), as you might expect, but also "God in man" (7.2).[12] This Lord "will be within us as our God—as he actually is" (15.3). Further: "For our God, Jesus the Christ, was conceived by Mary, in God's plan being sprung both from the seed of David and from the Holy Spirit. He was born and baptized that by his Passion he might hallow water" (18.2). In a textually obscure place Ignatius seems to speak of "[our] God, Jesus Christ" (Trallians 7.1) but he speaks of "the Christ God" (Smyrneans 10.1) unequivocally and "Jesus Christ, our God" (Romans, prologue). Elsewhere, his christology is couched in familiar New Testament terms.

Is Ignatius a doctrinal innovator, going beyond the affirmations of the New Testament? He is more likely drawing on liturgical phrasing from hymns in his home church that were being sung while the canonical collection was being completed. The faith of the churches in Jesus Christ, it must be remembered, was developing along more than one front. This same Ignatius was strongly anti-docetist, taking advantage of many occasions to stress Jesus' human flesh and the actual shedding of his blood.

A homily from the first half of the second century (in Egypt?) became associated with the name of Clement and is known as his Second Letter. It is addressed to gentiles and warns them sternly against a gnostic outlook. This sermon contains the first citation of a New Testament passage as Scripture (2.4, referring to Matthew 9:13; Mark 2:17; Luke 5:32). The author begins by saying that "we ought to think of Jesus Christ as we do of God—as 'the judge of the living and the dead' [Acts 10:42]," the Christ who endured much suffering for us (1.1-2).[13] We came to know the Father through him (3.2).[14] Of the incarnation it says: "If Christ the Lord who saved us was made flesh though he was at first spirit, and called us in this way, in the same way we too in this very flesh will receive our reward"

---

[12]Cyril C.Richardson, tr. and ed., *Early Christian Fathers* (New York: Macmillan, 1970), pp. 88, 89, 90.

[13]*Ibid.*, p. 193.

[14]*Ibid.*, p. 194.

(9.5).[15] Jesus is called not only the Savior in this homily but also "the prince of immortality" (20.5).[16] In it, too, a religious person looks forward to "the immortal fruit of the resurrection" rather than a reigning with Christ in the last age. The new Christian hope is that, "He will live again in heaven with his ancestors, and will rejoice in an eternity that knows no sorrow" (19.4).[17]

Justin, a Palestinian gentile, wrote his *First Apology* in Rome ca. 155. He is evidently struggling for a vocabulary to speak of the mystery of Jesus Christ and settles on "the Son who came from the most true God" as someone to be worshiped and adored (6),[18] the Word whom God begot (12).[19] "Jesus Christ alone was really begotten as Son of God, being his Word and First-begotten and Power, and becoming man by [God's] will he taught us these things for the reconciliation and restoration of the human race" (23).[20] "He is the Reason (*Logos*) of which every race of humanity partakes" (46).[21] He is called "Angel" and "Apostle" because he is both a messenger and one sent (63).[22] In his subsequently written *Dialogue with Trypho*, Justin calls the Word "a second divine entity and Lord" (*deuteros theos kai kyrios*) below the Creator of the universe, in arguing that the story of Abraham's visitors in Genesis 18 demands of Jews belief in such a one (IV. 56).[23] Justin in other places does not distinguish clearly between the Word and the Spirit, so it is evident that the Christian body is still in search of ways to speak of how God has been self-manifested lately in the life of Jesus and the Church. Yet the eucharist can confidently be called "the flesh and blood of the

---

[15] *Ibid.*, p. 196.

[16] *Ibid.*, p. 202.

[17] *Ibid.*

[18] *Ibid.*, p. 245; see 12., p. 248 and 13., p. 249.

[19] *Ibid.*, p. 248.

[20] *Ibid.*, p. 257.

[21] *Ibid.*, p. 272.

[22] *Ibid.*, p. 284.

[23] R.P.C. Hanson, ed., *Justin Martyr's Dialogue with Trypho, A Jew* (London: Lutterworth, 1963), p. 36.

incarnate Jesus" (1 Apology 66), an offering of thanksgiving, praise and glory "to the Father of the universe through the name of the Son and of the Holy Spirit" (65).[24]

This review of second-century answers to the question of who Christ is can be fittingly concluded with a creedal affirmation found in *The Refutation and Overthrow of the Knowledge* [*Gnosis*] *Falsely So-Called* of St. Irenaeus of Lyons, written ca. 180. Early in his first book of five he presents the creedal statement that the church received from the apostles and their disciples its faith in "one Jesus Christ, the Son of God, who was flesh for our salvation" who will come "from the heavens in the glory of the Father to restore all things, and to raise up ... the whole human race, so that ... every tongue may confess him and he may execute righteous judgment on all" (I.10).[25] In attacking the various gnostic systems, his special target, he points out that in their creedal statement, "they always bring in the Word of God and the Christ who is from above as without flesh and free from suffering. Some think that he was manifested as a transfigured man, but say that he was neither born nor incarnate. Others say that he did not even take the form of a man, but descended like a dove on that Jesus who was born of Mary" (III.11).[26] Against all these and even more bizarre positions—like Jesus' passing through Mary "like water through a tube" and his descent, by dispensation, on the son of the Demiurge—the Syrian missionary to Gaul shows them to be false witnesses by quoting the fourth gospel: "And the Word was made flesh and dwelt among us" (1:11).

A French professor of the New Testament has assembled a set of texts from the first four Christian centuries, starting with Jewish prayer and proceeding through doxologies, blessings and hymns from the New Testament (set in type as poetry), to various euchologies of the churches of Egypt and Syria, Greece

---

[24]Richardson, p. 286.

[25]*Ibid.*, p. 360.

[26]*Ibid.*, p. 379.

and Rome.[27] It is perhaps a more important collection than those which contain or summarize theological treatises because it conveys the prayer forms used by hundreds of thousands as contrasted with the learned tomes available to hundreds. In these prayers of praise of God and thanks for salvation through Jesus Christ in the Spirit, no limit is put on the intimacy of Christ with God. Identity and distinction between the two are often affirmed in the same phrase without any attempt at resolution of the paradox. At the end of a careful review of all these prayer forms one can only conclude that the person who emerges is the one, undivided Jesus Christ who is simultaneously true God and true man. He is at the same time one whom a subtle mind can dissect or separate if its starting point is the total incommensurability of deity and humanity. One who is previously convinced that creaturehood can be the manifestation or agency of the creator God, but can in no sense be united in substance to that God, will find ways to explain that the various scriptural affirmations cannot mean what they say. The unity of God and man in one person is a clear impossibility to anyone who starts with the conviction that it is impossible.

To others like Melito of Sardis, who wrote a regrettably anti-Jewish but in other respects sublime hymn *On the Pasch* (second half of the second c.), this non-nuanced phrasing came rolling from his pen like billows following one upon another:

> For it is I who am your forgiveness,
> I, the saving Pasch,
> I, the Lamb sacrificed for you,
> I, your purification, I, your life,
> I, your resurrection, I, your light,
> I, your salvation, I, your King!
>
> It is I who bring you
> to the heights of heaven;

[27]Lucien Deiss, C.S.Sp., tr. Matthew J. O'Connell, *Springtime of the Liturgy. Liturgical Texts of the First Four Centuries* (Collegeville, MN: Liturgical Press, 1979), pp. 307.

it is I who shall raise you up here on earth.
I will show you the eternal Father,
I will raise you with my right hand.

Such is he who made heaven and earth,
who in the beginning fashioned humanity,
who was foretold by the Law and the prophets,
who took flesh in the Virgin,

who was hanged on the tree,
who was buried in the earth,
who was awakened from among the dead,
who ascended to the heights of heaven,

who sits at the Father's right hand,
who has the power to judge and save all,
through whom the Father created all things
from the beginning to eternity. . . .

He is risen from among the dead,
he sits at the Father's right hand,
he possesses the Father and is possessed by the Father.
To him be glory and power forever! Amen.[28]

---

[28] Deiss-O'Connell, pp. 109-10.

2

Where Did Jesus' Followers Get the Idea They Needed to be Redeemed?

Before we launch on an inquiry into Jesus' role as the savior or redeemer of the human race—a concept that is central to the gospel—it might be helpful to know where it came from. Did Jesus ever present himself as someone whom the world could look to for redemption? Did the Jewish people into which he was born "await a redeemer" or "look for salvation," as is so often said? And, whatever the answer to this second question, who is mainly responsible for placing the idea of redemption dead center in the preaching of the gospel?

Christian evangelism in the West assumes three forms chiefly, the Catholic (the main outlines of which many in the Anglican and various Protestant communions identify with), the classic Reformed in its Lutheran, Calvinist or pietist mode, and the "evangelical" (necessarily a redundancy when evangelism is spoken of)—what may be called right-wing Calvinism of the kind this country has exported through mission effort worldwide.

God the Redeemer of Israel

The starting point of all Christian theologies of redemption is the conviction that God is the deliverer (or rescuer) of humanity from its plight, as at first was—and is—the case uniquely for the people Israel. Until late in this century few

Christians would permit the phrase "and is." Few enough do today. The conviction has been widespread among Christians from A.D. 150 onward that, ever since the close of the apostolic age, God has had no special concern for the Jewish people such as the Bible depicts. That conviction recedes in some quarters ever so slowly, in others not at all. It is right to identify as the starting point the biblical image of YHVH as the *go'el* of Israel, the one who would pay the ransom price if it were taken captive (the literal meaning of redemption) or "bail it out" of any extremity. Israel thought it was good to have a friend like that. The first great test had come with the deliverance from Egypt in Moses' day. A second, like it, was the restoration from Babylonian exile which caused one of the biblical poets to write: "I will help you, says the LORD; your Redeemer is the Holy One of Israel" (Isaiah 41:14b). This was a great deliverance in the prophet's eyes, greater indeed than anything that had gone before. He wrote, speaking for YHVH:

> Remember not the things of the past,
>   the things of long ago consider not;
> See, I am doing something new!
>   Now it springs forth, do you not perceive it? (43:18-19a).

In fact, the release from Babylonian exile never eclipsed the earlier rescue from Egypt in the popular imagination. The people of Israel did, however, devise a concept of creation on the basis of this re-creation which it worked into a poem (1:1—2:4a) and a story (2:4b—3:24) in early Genesis.

If a Christian of today were to ask a Jew of Jesus' day, "Have you been saved?" the Jew might be expected to ask what the question meant. After a patient explanation—which could go misunderstood because of its Christian vocabulary of sin, guilt and death—the now informed Jew might answer that if "saved" meant rescued or ransomed, of course he was—at the hand of the LORD by being brought through the Red Sea. "Yes, but were you saved personally as a result of a faith in God like that of Abraham?" After a blank stare and a series of questions for clarification, the answer would probably come: "It did not happen to *me*. It happened to *us*, to all Jews. We are a saved people, for whom any other rescue like that from

Babylon is but an echo. And we hope to be saved by our God on the last day." He is a Jew of Jesus' day, remember, not ours. That last response does not have a modern ring.

This hypothetical conversation is a way of showing how very Christian redemption is in the form in which Christians have cast it. It might also help to point out how meaningless the question "Are you saved?" is to a *modern* Jew—only slightly more meaningless than to a first-century Christian, who would answer: "But of course. The whole Church is saved!"

Jews and Muslims are likely to tell Christian questioners concerned for their souls' salvation that they have no teaching about human sinfulness from which they need redemption. Christians seem to think that they should. Of course, these others know about the universality of death. But they do not connect it with any primordial sin, only with the will of God ("the decree of Allah") in humanity's regard. In both traditions there is the certainty that God has acted as a teacher through revelation, who has given people the freedom to obey or disobey. Neither Jews nor Muslims are Pelagians in the Christian sense, viewing humans as needing no divine assistance to make their virtuous choices. But they do not speak in the same terms as Christians of the mysterious interplay between human and divine agency. Both are quite sure that, whereas *they* believe in human freedom, Christians do not. Or else they think Christians believe their liberty to be so unalterably maimed that only God's intervening action can deliver it from the weakened condition to which it is reduced. There is a puzzlement bordering on contempt shown by these two families of believers for the poor view they think Christians have of human capability. The Jew and the Muslim yield to no one in their conviction about the power of God, but they find the human creature in Christian eyes strangely unempowered by God. Relative to what God does for it apart from human action, they think Christians believe human nature can do nothing. In a word, the Christian belief in the weakening power of sin—Adam's sin, which in its effect on us is called "original"—is something that appears to have no counterpart among others who say they revere the same Scriptures as we. They would find in the Jewish pseudepigraphic writings but one account of Adam's fall in which "we sinnèd all." It occurs in 4 Ezra (2 Esdras) 7:116-18, an apocalyptic work, and says that Adam's sin caused our downfall. The position was not taken up by subsequent Jewish thought.

The Human Part in Human Redemption

An important starting place for this discussion, therefore, is why what is axiomatic for the Christian is such for no one else. Other questions of consequence are whether all Christians have the same faith when it comes to a need for redemption and how redemption is given. Many readers may not have encountered the phenomenon, but most evangelical Christians think that Catholics are no better than Jews in supposing that they can achieve their own redemption. They thereby stigmatize not one tradition but two. Some members of the Reformation churches think the same, namely that St. Paul's reprobated "works of the law" are what Catholics refer to as "meritorious acts." These religious battles of the sixteenth and seventeenth centuries had largely fallen dormant by the mid-twentieth except in places like the Reformed churches of Northern Ireland and South Africa. The aggressive evangelicalism of the last few decades has revived them in their most pronounced form.

What are the elements in this debate—not so much between Christians and others as between confessions or parties of Christians? One strong element is whether the human will is free or simply appears to be. Has God given the creature liberty of choice which can be exercised against both the creature's best interests and godhead itself? Or is the divine will so sovereign that it cannot let itself be thwarted, having ultimately to prevail over the creature whatever appearance of freedom is given? Another element is the measure of human activity that is to be credited in the acceptance of the gift of salvation God holds out. Has humanity any part in the divine redemptive deed which can properly be called its own? Or is it God's work from start to finish, with the human will simply fortified to acquiesce in it? A third element is the means by which the benefits of redemption are made available to the

Christian. Is it by an act of faith in the gospel heard or read, the outward sign of which is baptism? And as to baptism, how essential is it? Does faith alone achieve the redeemed status which the symbol of water signifies or does the water also effect it?

That is part of a larger question, does God stand ready to accept or justify individual new believers on their own or does the believing community play an essential role in their being redeemed? That is a way of introducing the question of a Church with sacraments and a sacrificing priesthood acting as a divine intermediary. Is there any such thing, or do stories like those told in early Acts, minimally interpreted, provide all the guidance we need: a proclamation of God's deed in raising Jesus up from the dead, a challenge to faith in that deed followed by an invitation to approach the symbolic water, whereupon the fullness of Christian life begins without the need of intermediaries of any sort, not even the ministry of a baptizer? Since all who adopt any of these positions look to the Bible as their source, it is evident that the way various Christians resort to the Bible is basic to their theories of redemption. At this point, it should be evident, a consideration of the biblical sources is essential.

In Jesus' day, all Israel looked to the LORD as its king and sole deliverer. The Bible has the general conviction that humanity is sinful but thinks it possible for the Jew to be righteous or just (*tsaddiq*) by faithful fulfillment of the terms of the covenant found in the law. So the rabbis taught, basing themselves solidly on the Scriptures but chiefly the five books of Moses. They did not make much of the Adam story in Genesis, least of all identify it as the revealed account of the origins of human sin. They were more inclined to stress the "aggressive drive" (*yetzer ha rah*) as the cause of human evil if it is not curbed, and in postbiblical days the baleful influence of the devil. Humanity generally was thought to be impelled by a "tendency toward good" (*yetzer ha tov*). The LORD had made a human creature who was capable of either doing what was fitting or failing to. Nowhere in the Bible is human freedom questioned. Neither is it ever supposed that there is a basic incapacity to do what is right. Those writings are familiar with God's graciousness (favor) to suppliants, but they do not posit God's "grace" as necessary for making a right choice.

The Teaching of the Gospels
on Redemption Through Christ

In Jesus' day the Jewish people entertained the lively hope
that their God would deliver them soon from the oppressors
who bound them. The LORD who was king would do this.
Some favored violent means to assist the providential hand,
others total passivity. A definitive inbreaking was envisioned
in which the LORD would in fact reign and Israel would rejoice
in the rule. Usually described as "messianic expectation" or
"eschatological hope," this was the popular mood that Jesus
built upon to propose the correct terms of the "reign of God."
The concept was biblical in that YHVH and no other was
Israel's deliverer. It was postbiblical in the measure that this
people looked for final deliverance as an *impending* reality. As
to the terms of the reign of God ("kingdom of Heaven," in the
avoidance of the divine name favored by Matthew), God had
set them long ago in Torah. Jesus' teaching merely indicated
the kinds of righteousness which the one he called "my Father"
looked for and not a false conception of righteousness. He
preached future, even present, deliverance for those who would
keep the covenant faithfully. Jesus called it the rule of God (in
the gospels *hē basileia tou theou*). He never presented himself
as the redeemer of Israel. Only "my heavenly Father" was cast
in that role. He was completely confident, however, that his
terms for being ready for the onset of God's reign—to which
he never assigned a time or season—were the right ones.

As we read his teaching in the first three gospels we see that
he raised no question of whether people could do the Father's
will. Jesus assumed that they could. Only in John do we find
him saying: "No one can come to me unless the Father who
has sent me draw him, and I will raise that one up on the last
day" (6:44). Centuries later St. Augustine would build an
edifice of the necessity of "first grace" on this saying of Jesus.
In context it is more a matter of the Son's working in perfect
concert with the Father to achieve all the works of God than it
is a proof that God must be active in the achievement of every

human good. But it does somehow say the second as well as the first. Jesus the Jew would have confirmed the Johannine theology. God is in every human act that touches on the divine relation with the people of God's special concern. But every human act, being human, is free. A denial or even the slightest impugning of the freedom of the will is far from the spirit of Jesus. He is reported as inimical to the idea of slavery to sin (John 8:33). That *is* a bondage of the will. But from Jesus in the first level of gospel sayings we hear no mention of the need of God's gracious assistance for every action related to the pursuit of the kingdom ("salutary," in a later vocabulary). When he speaks of God's reign he envisions it as God's doing, not a human accomplishment. Being ready for it, however, living as if it had already arrived, most certainly is a human accomplishment. Jesus has no problem about whether people can accept the offer of life under God's rule which is held out to them. He thinks they can and must.

God is the redeemer of humanity in the synoptic gospels, we have said, not Jesus. John's gospel is more developed theologically than the others although not necessarily written at a late date. In one place that evangelist has the Samaritan towns-people of Sychar say that they know that Jesus "truly is the Savior of the world" (4:42). As in the rest of this gospel we have here the faith of the Johannine church. Jesus' task as savior is carried out by his doing everything the Father has commanded him (see 14:31). Returning to the synoptic gospels, they are interestingly very slow to tell us what value they put on Jesus' death and resurrection, which they all report at considerable length. They seem to assume that believers will know what to make of Jesus' final days and new, risen life. They do not put these above his words and deeds as Paul does by his silence about them. Twice only St. Mark, the first to write a gospel, tells us cryptically what he thinks this life and death achieves. In a section on the folly of the disciples' seeking power and position when their lot is immersion in pain, he has Jesus say: "Whoever wishes to rank first among you must serve the needs of all. The son of man has come not to be served but to serve—to give his life as a ransom for the many" (Mark 10:44-45). Service is Jesus' calling—as in the foot-washing episode of John 13:1-17—and the form it takes is the figurative payment of a purchase price (*lytron*) for release from captivity. The second overt Marcan statement of what is taking place with Jesus' death comes in the liturgy of the meal which Mark quotes, doubtless derived from the usage of his local community: "He said to them: 'This is my blood of the covenant which is to be poured out for the many'" (14:24).

Pairing the two texts, Jesus' life is being identified as the ransom price to set a people free, his blood the symbol of covenant renewal. Previous to these direct statements there has been Jesus' constant release of the afflicted and the possessed from their chaotic condition as order and peace are put in its place. Jesus is described, in his glorious coming, as the symbol of the triumph of God at the last day (13:26; 14:62). He is mockingly tagged "King of Judea" (15:2, 12), even as God is properly called King of Israel. The curtain of the sanctuary is torn in two as he dies (15:38), symbol of the end of one epoch and the start of another. Mark describes the beginning of the new life as "seeing him . . . in Galilee" (16:7). For this evangelist, Jesus has achieved for all who will suffer with him the inaugural of a new existence. It anticipates a final epoch of being with the glorified one.

None of the evangelists brings the description of the new life Jesus' deed accomplishes much farther than Mark. Matthew follows Mark exactly in the use of the ransom saying (20:28) but Luke, upon leading up to it (22:24-27), mysteriously omits it. Possibly this is because he has used the cognate word for ransom, *lytrōsis*, twice in other contexts (1:68; 2:38) to describe the deliverance already achieved by the birth of Jesus and the future setting free of Jerusalem. He will use the verb form again in 24:21: "We were hoping that he was the one who would set Israel free." Some, taking their cue from Rudolf Bultmann, have argued that Mark 10:45 is a church reformulation of the saying in Luke 22:27, but most are inclined to see in it a part of the primitive Marcan tradition. Matthew uses a snatch from the fourth servant song of Isaiah, as Mark has not done, to convey that in Jesus' exorcisms and healings he is achieving a great benefit for the many:

> It was our infirmities he bore, our sufferings he endured (Matthew 8:17, quoting Isaiah 53:4).

That poem is about the improvement of the lot of a whole people because of a mysterious sufferer ("the chastisement that made us whole; by his stripes we were healed ... he was smitten for the sin of his people," vv. 7, 8). It is probably right to see in Matthew's use of it in a context of Jesus' cures a similar intent. The passage may also be echoed in Matthew 26:63, Jesus' silence before his questioners (cf. Isaiah 53:7), just as Matthew 26:28 (= Mark 14:24) probably means to reproduce Isaiah 53:12 in speaking of blood poured out for the many. Unquestionably the healing narratives of Matthew, Luke and John are meant to portray Jesus as the deliverer from the miseries of the present eon, marked by death and sin. His promise of the kingdom is the dawn of a new age for humanity. By being raised up from the dead, only he lives the life of God's reign in its fullness, but he has shown the way.

"I go to prepare a place for you, and then I shall come back to take you with me, that where I am you also may be" (John 14:3). There is a unique, present quality to the treatment of God's rule in the fourth gospel. John knows and retains the apocalyptic tradition of the complete deliverance of Israel in the future, but his "eternal life," already begun, is the most anticipated mystery of redemption of the four. All the evangelists name fidelity to Jesus' teachings as the one sure means of bringing about God's reign. John is distinguished by thinking it already here in Jesus' person. His Jesus is "the lamb of God who takes away (bears? carries?) the sin of the world" (1:29). Whoever has seen him has seen the Father (see 14:9). The life of the new age is launched for John with this vision of faith, this seeing Jesus.

The gospels, although written in Greek and in the diaspora, are witnesses to the faith of Palestinian communities. We have nothing else like them. They testify to the conviction that, with the resurrection of Jesus of Nazareth, the old eon is ended and the world to come is begun, not yet here but its presence assured. "From the fig tree learn a lesson, When its branch grows tender and sprouts leaves, you know that summer is here. Likewise, when you see all these things happening, you will know that he is here, standing at your door" (Matthew 24:32-34). The end-time future is one reality. The end-time present is another. The "present age" of Jewish apocalyptic was not something theorized on. It did not have to be because it was an everyday reality. A hard life of cruel land-rent schemes for the peasantry, defeat for the whole people by one pagan power after another, a life brutish and short for all, with death at the end. It is true that biblical Israel had no over-arching theory of sin which required universal redemption. But that is not to say that it did not know a deeply flawed human existence with death and the grave as the ultimate enemy. In its Maccabean-era faith in the resurrection it looked for the conquest of death on the last day. Israel lived in hope of victory over all its enemies by a Davidic conqueror-king to come. Jesus spoke to these frustrations and hopes in his preaching of the reign of God. He was nailed to a tree because despots fear all liberation movements, civil or religious. With the resurrection, the liberator was himself liberated. The life of a people ransomed from Egypt entered on a new phase. A tiny segment of it saw itself redeemed finally from sin and death by its God, the LORD, acting through one of its own number.

The Lucan Kerygma in Acts

One of the evangelists, Luke, was alone in producing a follow-up volume to his gospel. It is much argued whether this author of the Acts of the Apostles was known to St. Paul or, if not, was influenced by his teaching. Whatever the case, he presents a full-blown theory of human redemption such as is to be found in no gospel. This may be because only he sets himself to record the apostolic preaching. The others are at pains to repress it in their chosen technique of reporting only on Jesus' words and deeds in his lifetime. Luke composes a series of addresses by Peter in the early chapters of Acts, in the manner of historians of the time. We cannot know whether he possessed a "Jerusalem source" that guided him. Since all of his biblical quotations are from Greek translations rather than the Hebrew or Aramaic Peter would have used, the supposition is that he drew on apologetic sermons that had been preached many times in the diaspora. To account for the outpouring of the Spirit on the first Pentecost, for example, he uses an apocalyptic vision of Joel that featured such a gift on the "great and terrible day of the LORD," in which every one of the remnant on Mount Zion who "called upon the name of the LORD would be saved" (Acts 2:17-21, quoting Joel 3:1-5, NAB). The saving or rescue of the apostolic age, however, would not be from the cosmic catastrophe the prophet envisioned. It would resemble the rescue from death and corruption God had given to Jesus (Acts 2:24), foreshadowed in a snatch of a psalm, where the ancient poet had spoken only of the deferment of death (Psalm 16:8-11). Unlike David, whom death overcame, Jesus had been exalted at God's right hand and had poured out the Spirit he had received from the Father (Acts 2:29-33). The "saving" of this early preaching, therefore, was not a rescue of the just on the final day, as in Joel, so much as a snatching of Jesus from death's corrupting influence. This rescue from death will be replicated for those who believe in it, through the rich outpouring of the Spirit of God. In Lucan theology, repentance and a baptism for the forgiveness of sins must follow, "and you will receive the gift of Holy Spirit" (2:38). The "you" are the Jews to whom the promise was made and those "far off," a biblical reference to gentiles (v. 39; cf. Isaiah 57:19). The prophesied, suffering Messiah whom God has glorified continues to be central to the Lucan proclamation (Acts 3:13, 18; 10:40-43). Faith in this promised one will wipe away sins (3:19) and bring a "season of refreshment," the "time of universal restoration" which will culminate Jesus' stay in heaven (vv. 20-21). He is, meanwhile, the promised prophet like Moses (Deuteronomy 18:15, 18) sent to turn Israel from its evil ways (Acts 3:26).

Thus is redemption preached in this early tradition. It is "the resurrection of the dead in [the person of] Jesus" (4:2), of which the sign is the healing miracles performed by the apostles. Belief in the exalted Christ, to which the cross in Luke's thought is the prelude, brings all the benefits of the hoped for final age, even if not immediately. It is thus not surprising that faith in the suffering Just One, now in glory, is at the heart of Stephen's preaching (7:52, 56) and even that of Paul (13:16-41; 17:3, 30-31). We get the same Lucan *kērygma* everywhere, on whosever lips it is placed. Faith in the risen Messiah is at its center. Accepting this "fulfillment of every promise" will lead to the remission of sins and the upraising of the faithful on the last day for a season of endless glory.

The Difference Paul Made to Traditional Teaching

St. Paul wrote his extant letters well before the Acts of the Apostles—probably in the years 50-57. This means that consulting them for a theology of redemption, which would include the diaspora presentation of the gospel Paul received before he added his own insights, will take us as far back as we can go in the non-Palestinian sphere. It may be the earliest, absolutely, since the gospels and Acts—despite their sources from the heartland of Israel—give evidence of much development in Hellenist modes of thought. Paul was convinced that God had appointed the risen Christ as Lord and savior of the world. The gift of the Spirit is given to all who believe in Christ. Those who treasure it have it as a pledge or guarantee of future salvation. At present they participate in Christ's body (see 1 Corinthians 6:13b-18a; 10:14-22; 12:27) and are considered one Spirit with him (6:17; 12:13; 2 Corinthians 13:14). As servants of this Lord they are expected to act in accordance with the Spirit. Paul is sufficiently in the Jewish apocalyptic tradition that "salvation," while going on in the present, is always future for him, a deliverance from the divine wrath on the last day (see Romans 5:9;10:9; 1 Corinthians 5:5; 1:18; 2 Corinthians 2:15). Only once does he write that "we were saved [aorist, hence timeless, rather than a past tense] *in hope*" (Romans 8:24). This makes salvation effectively future. The passage in Colossians which says we are raised to life in him (2:12) seems to be a theological development of Paul's thought, as a passage in Ephesians (2:5-8) undoubtedly is. This means that, while St. Paul would readily acknowledge that baptized believers have been sanctified in the sense of cleansed (1 Corinthians 1:2) and transferred to the Lordship of Christ (Romans 14:8-9; 1 Corinthians 3:23; 7:22-23; 2 Corinthians 10:7), he would not say they "have been saved." In the same way, he calls members of his churches "believers" and "saints" but never "the righteous" as a title, although he does say they have been justified (Romans 8:30; 1 Corinthians 6:9-11; for "those justified," but not as a title, see Romans 2:13 and 5:9).

St. Paul adopts the widespread view that he finds in the tradition that Christ's death, being a sacrifice, was a propitiation, expiation or substitution (in the New Testament, *hilastērion*) for past transgressions. Like those who believed in Christ before him, he uses the standard sacrificial terms of temple practice but does not develop them. Thus, his basic interpretation of the death of Jesus is that of the Church which he entered: "For I handed on to you first of all what I myself received, that Christ died *for our sins* according to the Scriptures" (1 Corinthians 15:3). This was the primitive way of dealing with the scandal of a crucified Messiah, namely finding in Jesus' death a victimhood that was divinely ordained to achieve a benefit for the multitude. Romans 3:25-26 is an important text for Paul's adoption of the tradition: "God put [Christ] forward as an expiation by his blood, to be received by faith. This was to show God's righteousness, because in his divine forbearance he had passed over former sins ... it was to prove ... that [God] justifies the one who has faith in Jesus." And again: "It is in this that God proves his love for us: that while we were still sinners, Christ died for us. Now that we have been justified by his blood, it is all the more certain that we shall be saved by him from God's wrath." Since reconciliation was achieved by his death while we were still God's enemies, it is certain that we shall be saved by his life (see Romans 5:8-10).

The deutero- and trito-Pauline writings repeat the tradition of redemption (*apolytrōsis*) through Christ's blood for the remission of sins (see Colossians 1:14, 20; Ephesians 1:7; 2:13). Texts like these have led to the assumption that when Paul speaks of Christ's dying "for all" (*hyper pantōn*) he always has a sacrificial death for past transgressions in mind. But in 2 Corinthians 5:14-15 Christ's dying for all is not expiatory; rather it is a death for all that will mean their living for him. "One dies to the *power* of sin, and does not just have trespasses atoned for. It is probable that we should read Galatians 1.4 in the same way,"[1] with its declaration that Christ gave himself for our sins to deliver us from the present evil age. In both of the above cases, Paul has gone beyond identifying Jesus' death as expiatory for past sins and identified it as placing us in a new condition with respect to the eon over which he presides as Lord. This is expressed well in still a third passage: "Whether we live or whether we die, we are the Lord's. For *to this end* Christ died and lived again, that he might be Lord both of the dead and the living" (Romans 14:8*b*-9). These statements identify a purpose in Jesus' death that goes well beyond expiation for past transgressions.

Close attention to these Pauline texts indicates that the popular presentation of Christ's death in the churches often stops with what the apostle held in common with all New Testament soteriology. He believed, of course, that Christ died in our place, "sinless in the sinner's stead" as the Easter hymn says. But he enriched the earliest tradition marvelously in a way that is often lost. He asserted, looking forward more than backward, that the purpose of Christ's death was to assure life with him whether one is alive or dead at his coming. Subsequent Christian tradition laid hold of half of Paul's message: what Christ accomplished concerning the past, namely an elimination of the guilt of sin. But that choice was much influenced by the fifth-century Augustinian development which promoted Adam to the role of humanity's enemy in a way not quite intended by St. Paul. Paul was a man of the eons or ages. He saw Christ's leading of humanity into the new eon as the most important thing he did. The fading of apocalyptic interest in a gentile Church had much to do with making Paul's major thrust less than fully available to it. Instead, the Church let itself be distracted by second-century chiliasm, medieval millennialism and modern apocalypticism, all of which have in common straining at the imagist gnat and swallowing the literalist camel.

Paul's great contribution was to identify Christ's death as not chiefly cancelling former guilt but freeing from the power

---

[1]E.P. Sanders, *Paul and Palestinian Judaism* (Philadelphia: Fortress, 1977), p. 465.

of sin and death and leading into new life (see Romans 6:3-11; 7:4; Galatians 2:19-20; Philippians 3:10-11). In this venture, increased sanctification is given daily to those who accept the challenge of the new age. Christians share Christ's sufferings so as to share his life. The outcome is not assured. The divine deed which has reconciled (Romans 5:10-11; 2 Corinthians 5:18-19) or justified (1 Corinthians 6:11; Romans 5:9) was accomplished on Calvary and at the empty tomb. All praise to it, but this does not or should not result in the "calm confidence of the Christian with four aces." A certain way of presenting the gospel has made it that, but not the *kērygma* of St. Paul. *He featured the deed of God as leading to participation with Christ in the new eon.* This is a benefit that has to be laid hold of day by persevering day (see 2 Corinthians 4:10; 1 Thessalonians 1:6), now that one belongs to God.

Whoever participates in Christ's death now has the pledge of risen life in time to come. The world is at present "in bondage to decay" (Romans 8:21), in Paul's apocalyptic thinking. The law of the Spirit, however, has "set me free from the law of sin and death" (8:2). This means that believers have in prospect "the glorious liberty of the children of God" (v. 21). Transformation is going on every day (see 2 Corinthians 4:16) but its fullness lies only in the future with the Spirit as present guarantee (5:1-5). Everywhere, Paul writes as if what must be in the lives of believers has already taken place. It is clear, though, that he has no illusions. Transformation in Christ is as yet highly imperfect.

We have raised the question before of where Paul got the idea that all had sinned in Adam, since its one mention in a first-century C.E. apocryphal writing (4 Ezra 7:116-18) is accompanied by little indication from that period of widespread belief in it. Paul was probably in search of a figure for totality which made the progenitor of the entire race the natural choice. His starting point was Jesus as Savior and Lord, not the sorry condition the human race was in. But this meant he needed a polar opposite to Christ. Who but Adam? The rabbinic world in which Paul had a part was convinced of Israel's desperate condition at the hands of its pagan oppressors. It knew the extent of human sinfulness, far greater among the pagans than Israel, it thought, but universal even there. Israel had at least been told how to repent and make satisfaction for sins. But universal hereditary guilt formed no substantial part of Jewish thinking. This fact has brought the accusation that Paul was completely out of the rabbinic mainstream. His starting point, however, was not the universality of sin and death but the "acquittal and life for all" that Jesus' act of righteousness led to (Romans 5:18). This is not to say that the mortality of all or universal sinfulness never crossed Paul's mind, only that his thinking began with God's answer to the predicament that humanity was in and not the predicament itself. He writes sweepingly that "in Christ all shall be made alive" (1 Corinthians 15:22) and refers to "the reconciliation of the world" (Romans 11:15; cf. 2 Corinthians 5:19), but it is clear from his mention of those who "are perishing" (1 Corinthians 1:18; 2 Corinthians 2:15) that he does not think that all will possess the life held out. This is made clear in Romans 5:17 where one man's trespass led to the reign of death in all, but those will reign in life who "receive (i.e., accept) ... grace and ... righteousness."

If the contrast between the two eons is uppermost in Paul's mind—Adam serving as a foil for Christ rather than determining that a redeemer was needed—we have an important clue to the apostle's view of the law. The law for Paul the Jew was the major symbol of an age that had been succeeded in Israel. The resurrection of Christ had brought that eon to an end. Hence, its sole shortcoming was that it was not Christ. E.P. Sanders' discussion of the law and the human plight shows why, in Paul's thinking, the law could not accomplish what only faith could: God had set new terms for Jew and gentile alike to come over to God.[2] To grasp Paul's actual intent is to see the baselessness of Augustine's interpretation of Paul, promoted by the Lutheran reform, which holds that Paul found the law an impossible burden to bear or that he

---

[2]E.P. Sanders, "4. The law, the human plight, and the relationship of the solutions to it," *op. cit.*, pp. 474-511.

thought fulfillment of it led to boasting. Rather, it brought righteousness to the Jew who kept it faithfully, as Paul was convinced he had done (see Philippians 3:6). Paul is terribly harsh, however, toward those who would force it on his gentiles (see Galatians 3—5). He does not hesitate to call it a "dispensation of death" (2 Corinthians 3:7) because of its fittingness for the old eon but lack of fittingness for the new.

At no point, however, does Paul identify release from the law as a positive good of salvation. Had it not been succeeded by something better that could impart life (see Galatians 3:21), its excellence as an interim device would continue (Romans 7:12). Gentile Christians who have not taken the pains to read Paul's letters with care have erroneously concluded that he thought it a burden Israel was well rid of. He does not begin with an analysis of sin, as they seem to think, but with a conviction about the way to salvation. The movement of his thought was this: since Christ's death and resurrection are God's answer to the human plight, what must that plight not have been? If the law could have put Israel and even the gentiles in a right relation with God it would have. There would have been no need for Christ's death, that "gracious gift" (Galatians 2:21). But he did die. Therefore there must have been something the law could not accomplish. Paul starts out knowing that belonging to Christ is the only thing that leads to life. Participating in the death of Christ assures resurrection with him—that and nothing else (Romans 6:5). There is nothing wrong with law observance, nothing whatever, except that it does not fit this revealed formula. Sin consists only in not having as one's goal being found "in Christ" (Philippians 3:9). Consequently, all the thumpings delivered in Christian rhetoric to those who do not have faith, or who seek a righteousness based on the law, are misdirected if it is not seen that belonging to Christ is the chief matter at issue. Paul's sole concern is that "you can't get there from here," namely to fulfillment of the promise made to Abraham via any route but faith and *participation in* the cross and resurrection.

How are people, Jews or non-Jews, to be redeemed, in Paul's view? By hearing the "word of Christ." Have people heard it? He thinks that within a quarter century or so they have, Jews especially, because of his preaching efforts and those of others like him (Romans 10:14-18). This passage in Romans is a marvelous spur to missionary activity but it has left the church effectively without a theology of redemption of those who have not heard the gospel. Worse still, it has confused being familiar with Christians of any quality of life with hearing the gospel. How many oceans of ink have been spilled and miles of airwaves drenched with "spreading the word!" Yet the world goes unredeemed because the gospel has not been lived, the only effective way in the Spirit to elicit faith in others.

Narrowing the Pauline Message

The burden of the foregoing section is that believers have a powerful means of proclaiming redemption in the teaching of their great one Paul but have often settled for a caricature of it which stresses the peripheral over the central. "Faith in the deed of God in Christ as against any attempt to achieve one's own righteousness": so far so good. But, after that, a pummeling of the law of Moses, for which long dead Jews or their living descendants, or works-reliant Catholics, stand as surrogates, trivializes the Scriptures. The major offense is to disregard anything in Paul but his traditional view of Christ's death as substitutionary for past sins. But Paul had a relatively small concern with "sins" and a huge one with the epoch of "sin." Christians who deal with Paul in the above ways not only cut him down to their size but run the risk of presenting the profound mystery of divine invitation to a new life and free human response as if it were a commercial transaction. A benevolent God decides to forego wrath, the proper response to human transgressions. No matter that "wrath" is a technical term from Jewish apocalyptic that almost cannot be understood without a mastery of the total imagery of the end-time divine righteousness. In the popular presentation, God will disregard past offenses by accepting faith in the blood of Christ as legal tender. Put your trust in the cross and you have no further obligations, since God has done it all. Anything else is a human "work" no better than those reprehensible "works of the law." This version of the gospel of salvation is pitiful in the blunting of its fine Pauline edges—but many live by it for a lifetime. The apostle held out a rapier to his churches. Their descendants have hammered it into a broadsword.

What, then, did the man teach that is the church's largely disregarded treasure? He taught an intensely personal relation between God and Israel which was perceived as extended in Jesus' day to include the rest of the human race. Faith was the free human response to God's tender concern. The concern came first, however, not the response. God's deliverance from the human predicament came in the form of a human being who was uniquely God's son. How humanity, whether Jewish or gentile, would perceive its predicament was altered radically by the solution to it God held out in a human. The biblical authors had much to say about sin and death and divine deliverance, the pagan philosophers about ignorance and error, and knowledge as the key to immortality. Paul received the newly conceived tradition of Christ's death as the totally adequate sacrifice for past transgressions and handed it on. Whether he perceived a weakness in the imagery of the temple for his gentiles who had never experienced pilgrimage to Jerusalem, we cannot say. We do know that without repudiating Christ's death as a fulfillment of blood sacrifice he identified another, higher purpose for it. It was to achieve the transfer of a whole race of believers from the eon of death and sin to that of life and reconcilation, from the dominion of the "god of this age" who blinds, to the Lordship of Christ, "the likeness of God" (2 Corinthians 4:4).

Jesus Christ under God is the accomplisher of this transfer. It is God who can make of believers "one Spirit, one body in him" (canon of the Eucharist of the Roman Rite). Paul by this vision identifies himself as a man of the present and future, not simply the past. He recognizes that the blood of Christ has accomplished for all an expiation of sins which the sacrifices of the temple accomplished for individuals in Israel. But that settlement coped with the old eon. Christ's death and resurrection, more importantly, usher in the new. Together they make satisfaction for sins but do more, they break the hold of sin. The humanity that looks back to Adam is over, the humanity new in Christ that looks forward to his coming is begun. This second is not by any means a paradisal progeny. But it has the pledge of the Spirit, a gift to believers in the resurrection, which provides assurance that all God's promises will find their final Yes in Christ (2 Corinthians 1:20-22; 5:5; see also Ephesians 1:14). Believers in the resurrection can rise to their calling aided by "the Spirit who helps us in our weakness ... interceding for the saints according to the will of God," who "in everything works for good with those who love him" (Romans 8:26-28). This is the continuing graciousness (or grace) of God for Paul, a God who having reconciled (justified) a sinful humanity does not leave it on its own. Believers act constantly for or against their good while the Spirit acts with an even greater constancy, never deserting them. They belong, in a word, to Christ and this makes an immense difference in all they think or say or do.

Post-Pauline Views of Redemption

Whether Paul wrote Colossians or not, his view is perfectly captured in an early passage—note the priority—which says of Christ: "He has delivered us from the dominion of darkness and transferred us to the kingdom of his beloved Son, in whom we have redemption, the forgiveness of sins" (1:13-14). Again: "And you, who once were estranged and hostile in mind, doing evil deeds, he has now reconciled in his body of flesh by his death, in order to present you holy and blameless and irreproachable before [God], provided that you continue in the faith, stable and steadfast" (vv. 21-23*a*). First comes reconciliation, but for a purpose: presentation to God at the end of the age, provided that the new life of those who are Christ's intervenes (see 2:6-7).

The author or Ephesians had access to Colossians and probably wrote in the generation after Paul. He addressed himself unequivocally to gentiles. Ephesians shares with Colossians the imagery that says, "once you were darkness, but now you are light in the Lord; walk as children of light ... and try to learn what is pleasing to the Lord" (5:8-9). "Redemption through [Christ's] blood" is mentioned early in the treatise (which is hardly a letter): "the forgiveness of our trespasses" (1:7). The greatness of God's power "in us who believe" is the same as that which raised up Christ (vv. 19, 20), "making alive you who were dead through trespasses and sins" (2:1). The gentiles "who were once far off have been brought near in the blood of Christ," made one new creature with Israel in place of the two (v. 15), "members of the household of God" (v. 19), "a holy temple" (v. 21), "a dwelling place of God in the Spirit (v. 22). This is Paul's transfer language in other terms, describing the world of participation with Christ that follows the bringing to life of those who were dead through their sins (2:5). The word of truth was heard and belief followed; then came the seal and pledge of the promised Spirit (1:13-14; cf. 2 Corinthians 1:22). This tract, like Colossians and unlike Paul, uses the imagery of anticipated rule with Christ (2:5-6), which it calls "salvation," to describe the new life of the redeemed. The gentiles it addresses, having had a perilous career as hostile to God (2:16), "strangers and sojourners," have received a transfer of lordships. They have been made "fellow citizens with the saints and members of the household of God" (2:19). Clearly they are launched on the life of the new age.

It might well be asked if St. Paul's basically apocalyptic interpretation of redemption had any future, once that mode of thought became unavailable to a gentile church on terms true to the *genre* itself. "Transgressions" (*paraptōmata*) of torah or the law of nature are a daily reality. "Sin" (*hamartia*) as humanity's enemy personified is much harder to grasp. It is easy to consider the one the plural of the other and examine no further, assuming that Paul has pitted Christ against our sins rather than the apocalyptic reality Sin. As to getting a grip on a series of world epochs of which this is the last, that is bound to strike many as vain dreaming. "The form of the present world did not pass away, the end did not come and believers were not caught up to meet the Lord in the heavens."[3] Real participation in Christ, real possession of the Spirit are,

---

[3]Sanders, p. 523.

at the same time, ideas not readily separable from the cosmic matrix in which Paul first introduced them. They demand human solidarity as their basis or, if not that, at least the solidarity of church or people, ethnic group or worshipping community. Individualism set free from any sense of history cannot handle the Pauline construct based on peoplehood and linear time. The apostle was convinced that "Christ was appointed Lord by God for the salvation of all who believe, that those who believe belong to the Lord and become one with him, and that in virtue of their incorporation in the Lord they will be saved on the Day of the Lord."[4]

To handle a mythic concept like that only a powerful myth proper to every age will do. The reality of a worldwide community of believers, the one only Church, is such a myth. So is such a church at prayer, in liturgies as powerful as the temple sacrifice and pilgrimage feasts of Israel. (The same is true, *mutatis mutandis*, of the annual *hajj* of Islam, the *mahabharata* ["Great Epic"] of Hindu lore.) The church has such dramas in its eucharistic and other liturgies, many of them popular and unconfirmed officially. When performed as befits the burden they bear, they make corporate life in Christ real through feast and season. With the prospect of being saved on the Last Day the focal point, there is made real that life in Christ into which believers have been initiated by their great Champion. In that sense redeemed, they do not look back to his victory over their past sins so much as forward to fullness of the life his Father gave him in raising him up from the dead.

To scan the "pastoral epistles" to Timothy and Titus for the way they present the redemptive mystery is to find echoes of the master Paul. As Mark Twain said to his modest wife when she tried to cure him of his habit of profanity by producing a string of expletives of her own, "Effie, you've got the words but you don't have the tune." The pastoral epistles are often not in Paul's key but they sometimes say things fully in his spirit. Thus, when 1 Timothy says that "Christ came into the world to save sinners . . . those who were to believe in him for

---

[4] *Ibid.*

eternal life" (1:15-16) and that "there is one mediator between God and men, the man Christ Jesus, who gave himself as a ransom for all" (2:5-6*a*), he presents unimpeachable Pauline doctrine. One explicitation of Paul's teaching by this anonymous pastor stands out for the ages. He wrote that "God our Savior . . . desires all to be saved and come to the knowledge of the truth" (2:4). This universal salvific will of God became the church's faith despite Augustine's athletic attempts to limit it to mean that God desires all to be saved who will be saved. 2 Timothy captured the Pauline spirit accurately, even though the Hebrew resurrection of the dead had yielded to the Greek "immortality," in a hymn that sang of the power of God,

> who saved us
> > and called us with a holy calling,
> not in virtue of our works
> > but in virtue of his own purpose and grace
> which he gave us in Christ Jesus
> ages ago
> and now has manifested
> > through the appearing of our Savior Christ Jesus,
> who abolished death
> > and brought life and immortality to light through the
> gospel.
> (2 Timothy 1:9-10; cf. Titus 3:4-7)

The author, speaking for Paul, says he will "endure everything for the sake of the elect, that they also may obtain the salvation which in Christ Jesus goes with eternal glory" (2 Timothy 2:10). The hymn in the epistle to Titus cited immediately above says that when the goodness and kindness of God our Savior appeared, "he saved us . . . by the washing of regeneration and renewal in the Holy Spirit" (Titus 3:5). This figure of rebirth will appear as "being born anew" in 1 Peter 1:3 and 23.

The author of Hebrews takes a different tack from the Pauline school in developing his treatise-long contrast between Christ's final and effective priestly office and that of the high priests of Jerusalem's temple. He resembles the apostle, though, in describing Jesus as the trailblazer (*archēgos*) in bringing a great progeny to glory through suffering, "for he who sanctifies and those who are sanctified have all one origin" (Hebrews 2:10-11). This document, probably of Alexandrian provenance, is the strongest New Testament writing after John to feature the common life of the Savior and the saved: "Here am I, and the children God has given me (v. 13*b*, quoting Isaiah 8:18*a*). . . . Therefore he had to be made like his brethren in every respect, so that he might become a merciful and faithful high priest in the service of God, to make expiation for the sins of the people" (2:17). This propiatory office of the son of the household, not a servant like Moses, is featured throughout. The prize won by Jesus' priestly ministry is at times the "rest" (*katapausis*) in the promised land denied to some of the Israelites for disobedience (4:1). Again it is "eternal salvation" (5:9), and in one place enlightenment, a tasting of the heavenly gift which makes us "partakers of the Holy Spirit" and of "the goodness of the word of God and the power of the age to come" (6:4-5). This look to the present and the future resembles Philo in phrasing but it is like Paul in content. "Repentance from dead works" is identified as the foundation which no longer needs to be laid, as persons of faith move on to maturity. Repentance does not have to be repeated by those who have moved forward into the light (vv. 1-4).

In 2 Peter Jesus is called "Lord and Savior" four times, in 1 John "the Savior of the world" (4:14). 1 John knows the redeemed to be "children of God" now, without knowing what they shall be "when he appears" (3:1-2). 1 Peter quotes Hosea 2:23 to the effect that the baptized were once no people and are now God's people, recipients of God's mercy (2:10). This is preceded by referring Exodus 19:6 to them, expanding it to "a chosen race, a royal priesthood, a holy nation, God's own people" (1 Peter 2:9). The book of Revelation comes close by calling the baptized those whom Christ has freed from their sins by his blood and made a kingdom, "priests to his God and Father" (1:5-6; cf. 5:10). Other images of the new status of believers in that apocalyptic book are "those clad in white garments," the worthy whose names will not be blotted out of the book of life (Revelation 3:4-5; cf. 21:27). The Lamb, standing as though it had been slain, by his blood "ransomed people for God from every tribe and tongue and people and nation" (5:9). Those "who had been slain for the word of God" (6:9) come in for special attention in this book. They shall be rewarded above the baptized, whose blessed reward is also declared (14:13).

Perhaps the most striking use of a theology of successive ages in this book is to be found in two places, the one better known than the other. In the less featured of the two, loud voices in heaven say: "The kingdom of the world has become the kingdom of our Lord and of his Christ, and he shall reign for ever and ever" (11:15). This transfer of lordships is more complete than anything envisioned by Paul. The second, equally future in orientation, is a cluster of images rather than a single one: "the new Jerusalem, coming down out of heaven from God, prepared as a bride adorned for her husband" (21:2); a people that neither weeps nor cries out in pain any more (v. 4), a city that has "the glory of God as its light, and its lamp is the Lamb" (v. 23). There are twelve gates to the walls of this city, in turn set on twelve foundations (vv. 12-14) adorned with every jewel (vv. 19-20). "And its gates shall never be shut by day—and there, there shall be no night" (v. 25).

The Risen Christ: Starting Point for All Redemptive Faith

What, at base, accounted for the difference Jesus made to those who believed in him, however varied the religious rhetoric they employed to express it? Some say unfulfilled Jewish hopes of long standing. Others propose the ennui, the pointlessness of existence that gripped the ancient world. It was the biblical prophecies, still others suggest. Jesus fulfilled them exactly. A few say that apocalyptic expectation was the answer: it was the glove, Jesus the hand. A very few maintain that the Jewish consciousness of sin and the burden of removing it by successful acts of expiation were so great that there was a rush toward Jesus' invitation to a higher righteousness; this, Paul's attacks on the law confirmed. All these explanations are wide of the mark, some much wider than others.

It was the person of the crucified Jesus, experienced as risen by hundreds who knew him, who brought on the conviction that God had done something cosmic lately. What could it mean, they wondered? What was the significance of Israel's history in light of it? Could this be an answer to the question, so long deferred, of Israel's relation to the nations? To put these questions is to speculate on behalf of the apostolic band in ways it did not record. But the speculation is sound in placing the divine *factum* first and requiring all explanations to flow from it, not the other way around. There was no series of Jewish dilemmas being widely posed into which Jesus neatly fit, like the last piece in a puzzle. There was only the messenger's word, "He is risen. He is not here," to explode the conviction of many that only the just—and surely not the accursed impaled on a pagan stake—would rise on the last day. The resurrection of Jesus, alone and beforetime, as the Lord of life fit into no vision of the future then current, not even that of his closest friends.

It is from this fact of "the Living One" that all attempts to divide the ages into before and after grew: an Israel needing perfect expiation for its sins followed by that expiation accomplished; a people purchased, bought back from any power human or angelic that held it captive; a people profane and ungodlike now sanctified by its all-holy God, reconciled to the One with whom it had been at enmity, justified by the LORD of perfect righteousness. In light of this solution a host of human problems were identified. Past needs came to the fore, once the Christ was believed in who supplied for every lack. The condition of Israel, indeed of the gentile world and of the two in relation, was spoken of in terms never used before.

There was nothing traditional about the new situation—although the vocabulary of the Bible was used to describe it—because the event that triggered it was unique. We have to keep that in mind as we proceed. Nothing in the whole history of Israel, nothing in Graeco-Roman paganism or the lives of peoples on the farthest shores accounts adequately for the conviction of Christians that they were a people redeemed. It bore a certain correspondence to the life of the people Israel but, like that people, redemption as accomplished through Christ was something new under the sun.

3

The Doctrine of Redemption
in the Patristic Era

Albert Schweitzer began a chapter in 1906 which was to have served as the introduction to a book. The book got written and was published in 1911 under the German title *History of Pauline Research.*[1] The chapter was ultimately expanded into another book in 1931 entitled in English, as in German, *The Mysticism of Paul the Apostle.*[2] A career as a medical missionary in Lambaréné (modern Togo) in the years 1913-27 had intervened for the author. The preface to this book was written on shipboard as the Alsatian theologian returned to his mission hospital late in 1929. He maintained in this volume that a mystical dying and rising with Christ of the elect among Jews and gentiles was Paul's central teaching. Paul proclaimed to his gentile churches a transfer into the state of existence proper to the kingdom of God, a "belonging together" with our Lord in the final age which had already begun. Schweitzer thought this to be "the fundamental idea of the concept of redemption, which Paul worked out by the aid of the thought-forms of the eschatological world view."[3] But

[1] Albert Schweitzer, *Geschichte der paulinischen Forschung: Paul and His Interpreters,* tr. by William Montgomery, (New York: Macmillan, 1951).

[2] *Idem, The Mysticism of Paul the Apostle,* tr. by William Montgomery (London: Adam and Charles Black, 1931) (*Die Mystik des Apostels Paulus*). Reprinted in a *Seabury Paperback Edition* (New York, 1968).

[3] *Ibid.,* p. 380.

what Paul thus firmly grasped was later lost sight of. As the Church became increasingly Hellenized, a concept of redemption through Christ grew which was situated not within the rule of God that he proclaimed but, so to say, alongside it. Redemption began to be explained as if it were brought about by Christ's appearance in itself, no longer by his coming as the bringer of the rule of God. This so continued through the centuries that belief in redemption through Christ and belief in the reign of God never again formed a living unity. Schweitzer wrote:

> In Catholicism and in the Protestantism of the Reformers, both of which had their structure determined by the form which Christianity had taken in the process of being Hellenised, Christian doctrine is dominated by the idea of a redemption based upon the atoning death of Jesus for the forgiveness of sins, alongside of which the belief in the Kingdom of God maintains a not very vigorous existence.[4]

Schweitzer places the ineffectiveness of both Christian traditions during the Reformation period in their loss of belief in and desire for the "Kingdom of God in its original strength," a commitment which might have exerted a transforming influence on the circumstances of the time. While lamenting what did not happen, he points to the pietist movement in evangelical Protestantism between the end of the seventeenth century and the early part of the nineteenth as a place where belief in the rule of God attained powerful influence. He sees in just such successes, however, the paradox of a decline of any living concept of redemption through Christ. Among the heirs of "the redemption-religion of the Reformers," two pages later, he finds interest confined to

> the Pauline doctrine, understood in a thoroughly un-Pauline way, of justification by faith (which itself is only a fragment of a doctrine of redemption, owing its prominence to the controversy about the Law, not Paul's real doctrine of

[4]*Ibid.*, p. 381.

redemption), and proceeds, by the aid of ingenuous arguments, to erect into a principle the one-sidedness from which Christianity has suffered since its Hellenisation.

These powerfully expressed opinions share in the early twentieth-century outlook that has been characterized in Orwellian language as "Hebraic—good; Hellenic—bad." They also reflect the conviction, perhaps romantic, that non-Semitic generations of Christians were capable of absorbing "belief in and desire for the Kingdom of God in its original strength," presumably meaning mythic dress. The fact is that from the pastoral epistles and especially Ephesians onward there was the felt need to transpose the gospel into the cultural key of the Graeco-Roman world where it was increasingly finding a home. Still, Schweitzer's charge is a serious one and by no means unsupported by the facts. It is important for Christians to ask if the Church possessed a treasure in the primordial period which it mislaid or failed to utilize at full strength after that time. That treasure is redemption in the blood of Christ from human sinfulness, coupled with a transfer from the kingdom of darkness into the marvelous light of the rule of God, in a unity that in Schweitzer's view they enjoyed only in Jesus' kingdom-preaching and Paul's development of that theme, joining this transfer to Christ's expiation of transgressions by his sacrificial death. The modern trumpeting of "a fragment of a doctrine of redemption," "thoroughly un-Pauline," is so familiar to the Protestant and Catholic ear that it alone should supply motivation to explore whether an original richness in gospel preaching, namely union with Christ in the new age, was diluted at an early date.

In Chapter 2, we explored something of the variety of hymnic phrases, titles and arguments employed by the New Testament writers to describe the difference Jesus made to humanity, in particular those who believe in him. Whether or not, like Paul and the gospels with their pervasive apocalyptic tone, they divided human history into eons, they all looked on him as determining a "before" and "after," both in Israel's history and the life of all in this world. Whatever their views of humanity as sinful, the cosmos as out of joint, the devil as dominant in human affairs or darkness and ignorance as prevailing everywhere, they were at one in maintaining that God had employed Jesus as the totally free agent of the divine purpose to bring any who freely accepted him into a new condition. Even though the transfer was accomplished by the divine election of individuals and their reciprocal response to God's action it was basically corporate: from a peoplehood conceived on one set of terms to a new peoplehood entailing both continuity and discontinuity with the old. None of the figures of speech employed to describe the new condition of believers was considered fully adequate, hence the proliferation.

We must remember that, with a few exceptions like the interchange of the gospels among the Christian scribal class, the people of the early generations were not hearing the writings of the other churches read out in the assembly as they produced their own. A New Testament canon lay well in the future. Hymnodists and evangelists, the producers of correspondence and of articulated tracts, had as their common basing-point the risen Christ. He it was who invited the earliest disciples of both sexes to share in his new life. What Christ was with respect to God they too could be, if not immediately or with the same total intimacy with the divine, at least in good measure now, and in an unimaginable fullness later. They could transcend their previous limitations—the burden of their transgressions, ignorance of things of the spirit, the darkness of the present age, spiritual ruin, powerlessness before Satan or "the god of this world," the prospect of death without hope—and launch on a new existence variously described as life in Christ, knowledge, love, the remission of sins and anticipation of the Lord's coming, hope of the resurrection, reconciliation with God and neighbor, justification or a share in God's righteousness, light or enlightenment, the blessedness of God's rule/reign/kingdom; likewise salvation, sanctification, regeneration. life and immortality, redemption. Dominant in all these descriptions of the changed situation is the newness of the baptized and the God in Christ who is responsible for it. Their previous Jewish or Jewish and gentile condition, while something they are aware of, is not to the fore. A humanity in despair has not gone in search of a solution and found it in the life, death and resurrection of Jesus. It was the man Jesus who is Son of God now in glory who forced believers in him to articulate their previous condition. The view of that condition in retrospect was thoroughly influenced by the new faith. Any rabbinic thinker or pagan philosopher or even slave could say of the Christian retrospective vision: "That is not the way it was." Only faith in the way it *is* can say what believers in Christ are convinced they have been redeemed from.

The Judaism of the pre-70 rabbis, as is well known, looked for deliverance by God its savior from its situation of oppression through its faithfulness to the precepts of the covenant. A popular movement that originated before Jesus' lifetime had added oral precepts to the written precepts of Torah, a "hedge around the law." Covenantal fidelity in this twofold form was not basically at odds with another hope—one that looked for imminent deliverance and inauguration of the age to come: by patient, persevering waiting as the Pharisees saw it, by violent initiative under the banner of the LORD in the Zealot view. There was widespread expectation of "the days of Messiah," a hope we know about in the first century chiefly from the New Testament writings and the late first-century Jewish historian Josephus. Subsequent references to the idea in Mishnah and Talmud would confirm it. By any reckoning it had to be called the redemption of Israel.

Concurrently in the pagan world philosophers were teaching a lofty morality; one God over all or a unique principle called the All or the One; some even taught a survival of the soul after this life. A few like Plato's Socrates took on the popular religion of gods and goddesses as corrupting the morals of youth, but most were wary of a direct challenge of anything so cherished by the masses. In the first centuries before and after the Common Era the mystery religions, so-called, were enjoying an immense popularity. These featured an intimate, personal tie between devotee and protective deity. The individual pagan would be inducted into the mysteries ("hidden things") of a god or goddess—e.g., Cybele, Isis, Mithras—at the appropriate shrine, profess fealty to this deity of choice, and often return annually to the sacred spot to reenact in imitation (*mimēsis*) the deity's victory over death, the underworld, the grip of winter or infertility—whatever it might be. The great enemies to human happiness in the popular mind were two: the capriciousness of the gods of Olympus who were as likely to be unfriendly as friendly, and the more general power of *tychē* (*fortuna*) or *heimarmenē* (*fatum*) over their lives. The pagan world was in a constant struggle to outwit these forces, either uncertain or set against it. Private settlement via new cults of deities from the East was one such way. But paganism had no such protective covenant God as Israel did in the LORD.

Widespread in the first century A.D. was the Oriental religion of general gnostic cast (arcane *gnōsis* or "knowledge") which has much older roots than in Samaria-Palestine, initiated by Simon Magos, Menander, Satornilos and Basilides to whom the Christian fathers traced it. There was certainly an Iranian and Greek spirit-matter component to it going back several centuries. Its employment of biblical names and categories has influenced some to call gnosticism a Jewish heresy. This religion of obscure origins seems, however, to have displayed its chameleon-like character by the adoption of a Jewish guise as it infected Christian belief. No pagan religion called itself "Gnosticism." The name is the creation of modern historical scholarship. *Gnōsis* was, in fact, a quite respectable term for the knowledge revealed in Christ. Monks, intellectuals, and their Christian disciples would unashamedly call themselves *gnōstikoi*. As a challenge to the gospel, however, the religious system given this name was a potent one. "Gnosticism" proper was the late second-century religion which writers like Irenaeus of Lyons sought to unmask as having no place as an authentic expression of Christian faith. It may be defined as "a system which taught the cosmic redemption of the spirit through knowledge."[5] One such manifestation of it was led by Valen-

---

[5]Jaroslav Pelikan, *The Christian Tradition. A History of the Development of Doctrine* 1. "The Emergence of the Catholic Tradition (100-600)" (Chicago: The University of Chicago Press, 1971), p. 83. For a clear and dependable summary of the phenomenon, see Kurt Rudolph, *Gnosis. The Nature and History of Gnosticism* (New York: Harper and Row, 1987) tr. from 2d, rev. ed., 1980.

tinus who taught that,

> the perfect redemption is the knowledge of the ineffable
> Greatness itself. For weakness and suffering [come from]
> ignorance [while] knowledge is the redemption of the inner
> person. This is not bodily, since the body is corruptible; nor
> is it psychic, since the soul came from deficiency and is, as it
> were, a mere dwelling place of the spirit. So the inner
> spiritual person is redeemed by knowledge . . . of all things—
> and this is true redemption.[6]

Intimations of this gnostic spirit can be picked up in the
New Testament response to an exaggerated spiritualism (see
Luke 24:39; John 20:27; 1 John 1:1; 1 Corinthians 1:18—2:16,
15; Acts 17:32; 1 Timothy 5:23). It does not come clear as a
threat to Christianity, however, until the late second century.
In the non-canonical writings of the latter period, the increasingly gentile Church found itself presenting the gospel on
two fronts: against a polytheist paganism which, among the
learned, favored spirit over matter, and against a Judaism in
terms of which the Christian movement felt the need to define
itself. These two fronts of opposition, together with that of
Christians deviating from received understandings of Scripture,
resulted in a generally apologetic presentation of the new faith.
Despite this threefold need on Christianity's part, it is shocking
to see the early writers speak of Judaism and paganism almost
as though they were equally alien to the faith of the gentile
Church. They defended the stories of the Bible against pagan
criticism by saying that, however crude, these narratives could
not match the crudity and immorality of the Greek myths.
The apologists defended the unity and uniqueness of God with
the same arguments as their Jewish contemporaries. They also
dealt with the entire biblical deliverance as if its sole purpose
was to prepare for the coming of Christ.

The gospel is a message of salvation. There was unanimity

---

[6]Irenaeus, *The Refutation and Overthrow of the Knowledge Falsely So Called*
(*Adversus Haereses*), 1.21.4 in Cyril C. Richardson, tr. and ed., *Early Christian
Fathers* (New York: Macmillan, 1966), p. 366.

on that score. But there was no agreement on the meaning of the salvation proclaimed by this message. Whatever that meaning was, it never became a defined dogma of the Church. The earliest Catholic creed, adopted at Nicaea, said that "for the sake of us and for the purpose of our salvation" Christ came down and was made flesh, suffered, was raised on the third day, ascended, and will come as judge. Nowhere in this or later documents is it spelled out how the salvation which was the purpose of his coming was related to these events. Jesus' relation to God and to the human and divine within his person was dogmatically defined but never his saving work. Often in the christological debates it was affirmed that only a person who was truly God and truly man could have accomplished what he accomplished. Precisely what that accomplishment consisted in remained strangely unspecified. Yet it was from earliest times until now a core doctrine—even *the* core doctrine—of Christian faith.

An examination of the Church's teaching on Christ's work might be pursued by examining the major theories about his person or about the nature of sin, but both are unsatisfactory procedures. Pelikan in his history of doctrines proposes looking successively at what the early centuries made of Jesus' life and teachings, his suffering and death, and his resurrection and exaltation as the best way to discover what they made of the redemptive mystery.[7] That is the course we shall follow as we inquire into the teachings of the patristic age, remembering that none of the three developments ever appears in isolation from the other two.

Anyone who begins to look into the second-century writings convinced that only faith in the atoning death of Christ bespeaks redemption will be disappointed. Those authors saw many other aspects of his person and his deeds as achieving it. Clement of Rome (writing ca. 95), for example, reminds the leaders of the church at Corinth that they always stored Christ's words up carefully in their hearts and held his sufferings before

---

[7]Pelikan, *op. cit.*, p. 142.

their eyes.[8] Christ belongs to the humble, he reminds them, not the arrogant, coming in humility and shame, as the extensive quotations he provides of Isaiah 53:1-12 and Psalm 22:6-8 establish.[9] Clement concludes his brief chapter by saying: "You see, dear friends, what kind of example we have been given." Pelikan comments: "Precisely because salvation, however it may have been defined, was the fundamental truth of the gospel, the imitation of Christ as example and the obedience to Christ as teacher must be seen in their close connection with it."[10]

After a series of citations of the patriarchs and prophets as humble men preceding Jesus in the exercise of that virtue, Clement praises God's patient purpose and says something significant for any subsequent theory of salvation, since so many of them entail placating the divine wrath: "Let us consider how free from anger he is toward his whole creation."[11] There is condemnation in prospect if we "fail . . . to do what is good and pleasing to God."[12] But, he goes on to say to those who do what is acceptable to the creator God: "Let us fix our eyes on the blood of Christ and let us realize how precious it is to his Father, since it was poured out for our salvation, and brought the grace of repentance to the whole world."[13] This is followed, not long after, by: "Let us consider, dear friends, how the Master continually points out to us that there will be a future resurrection. Of this he made the Lord Christ the first fruits by raising him from the dead."[14] A kind and compassionate Father has made us his holy, chosen portion.[15] "We . . . who have been called by his will in Jesus Christ, are not

---

[8]Richardson, "The Letter of the Church at Rome to the Church of Corinth, Commonly Called Clement's First Letter" (2.1), p. 44.

[9]*Ibid.*, (16), p. 51.

[10]Pelikan, *op. cit.*, p. 143.

[11]Clement in Richardson (19.3), p. 53.

[12]*Ibid.* (20.1), p. 54; cf. p. 47 (7.3).

[13]*Ibid.* (7.4; cf. 36.1; 49.6).

[14]*Ibid.* (24.1).

[15]*Ibid.* (29.1; 30.1).

justified of ourselves or by our wisdom or insight or religious
devotion or holy deeds ... but by that faith by which almighty
God has justified all from the very beginning."[16] The author
presses the recipients of his epistle to obedience in order to
escape what God has promised the disobedient, so that these
who are humble "will be enlisted and enrolled in the ranks of
those who are saved through Jesus Christ."[17] An echo of Paul
on present justification and future salvation is discernible here,
not surprising in a letter coming from the city where he ended
his days. Faint echoes of the gospel tradition are also to be
heard—but, then, meditation on Jesus' life and teachings was
to be a staple of the Church's life.

In the *Teaching of the Twelve Apostles* (popularly the
Didachē, ca. 70-150) the opening moral precepts are identified
as the ways of life and of death and are described as "the
Lord's teaching to the heathen." The treatise then turns to how
to baptize, which must be preceded by public instruction, and
how to conduct the eucharist, giving thanks to the Father over
the cup and the loaf for having "revealed life and knowledge
[faith and immortality] through Jesus your *pais* (child? servant?)"[18] A prayer follows which asks God to bring the Church
from the ends of the earth into God's kingdom,[19] the final
redemptive benefit. Fragments in the prayers provided for
after the meal are spoken of in three successive verses as an
"offering" or "sacrifice."[20] They echo the Church's enduring
apocalyptic hope: "Let Grace [Christ] come and let this world
pass away" and "Our Lord, come." The second phrase is Paul's
maranatha of 1 Corinthians 16:22.[21]

An anonymous letter addressed to an equally unknown
Diognetus, perhaps the work of an early second-century
Platonist named Quadratus, speaks of God's having sent the

[16] *Ibid.* (32.4), p. 58.
[17] *Ibid.* (58.2), p. 70.
[18] *Ibid.* "The Didache," (9.3; 10.2), p. 75.
[19] *Ibid.* (9.4).
[20] *Ibid.* (14.1, 2, 3), p. 178.
[21] *Ibid.* (10.6), p. 176.

world's Designer and Maker to earth, out of kindness and gentleness, as God. "He [also] sent him as man to human beings. God willed to save humanity by persuasion, not by compulsion . . . he called people, but did not pursue them; he sent [Christ] in love, not in judgment. Yet God will indeed send him someday as our Judge, and who shall stand when he appears?"[22] The chief thing this "beloved Child" brought was knowledge of God which no one (presumably of the pagan world) had had before. For centuries God had patiently kept his wise counsel to himself as a well-guarded mystery. Then came "the present age of righteousness," a season for the manifesting of God's goodness and power in which he

> took up the burden of our sins [and] gave up his own Son as a ransom for us—the holy one for the unjust, the innocent for the guilty, the righteous one for the unrighteous, the incorruptible for the corruptible, the immortal for the mortal. For what else could cover our sins except his righteousness? . . . . The sinfulness of many is hidden in the Righteous One, while the righteousness of the one justifies the many who are sinners.[23]

A Plea Regarding Christians by Athenagoras, probably an Athenian philosopher of the last half of the second century, contains a strong confession of faith in the Father, Son or Word, and Holy Spirit as one in power but distinct in rank.[24] Through most of the treatise God's chief gift is a true knowledge of the cosmos which is not based on the mythic explanations of the pagans. Jesus is never mentioned by name nor called the Christ, neither is he identified as the giver of the benefit of the eternal life for which Christians hope:

---

[22]*Ibid.*, *The So-called Letter to Diognetus* (7.2-6), pp. 218-19.

[23]The editor and translator E.R. Fairweather (adapted) sees here echoes of Mark 10:45; 1 Timothy 2:6; Titus 2:14; "and above all Rom. 8:32ff." (8.1, 10; 9.1-5), pp. 219-21. Later (12.5), 1 Corinthians 8:1 will be attributed to "the apostle" (p. 223).

[24]*Ibid.*, ed. and tr. C.C. Richardson (10), p. 309.

When we depart this present life we shall live another. It will be better than this one, heavenly, not earthly. We shall live close to God and with God, our souls ... free from passion. Even if we have flesh it will not seem so: we shall be heavenly spirits. Or else, if we fall along with the rest, we shall enter on a worse life and one in flames.[25]

Already the Christian heaven and hell are in place, dislodging the apocalyptic hope of a blessed age to come or a rule of God on earth in which the wicked will not share.

If Athenagoras argues chiefly for belief in one God, the concern of the mid-second century apologist Justin is for acceptance of Jesus as the prophesied Messiah.[26] This gentile native of Samaria in Palestine made his circuitous way to Rome as a trained philosopher and rhetorician. Having become a Christian in adulthood, he there instructed others among the educated classes for baptism, giving private tutorial lessons in his lodgings. His *First Apology* (written ca. 155), like *First Clement*, tended to feature the purpose of the incarnation as chiefly didactic: Christ as teacher and example. This would be the first theme of the three described above as identifying the salvation Christ brought, namely the life and teachings of Jesus as a revelation of the truth. "The Word ... foretold that all these things would happen—our Teacher, I mean, who is the Son and Apostle of God.... We are sure that all the things taught by him are so, since we see that what he predicted is actually coming to pass."[27] To be a Christian is to live according to his teachings, "for he said that not those who merely profess but those who also do the works will be saved."[28] The life which is eternal and pure,[29] a living with God

---

[25]*Ibid.* (31), pp. 335-36.

[26]*Ibid.* "The First Apology of Justin, the Martyr," ed. and tr. E.R. Hardy (chs. 30-53), pp. 260-77.

[27]*Ibid.* (12), p. 248.

[28]*Ibid.* (16), p. 252. Much of chs. 15-17 are devoted to Jesus' "short and concise sayings" from Matthew and Q (Matthew and Luke in near-identical wording).

[29]*Ibid.* (8), p. 246.

in incorruption of the body and fellowship[30] will follow such fidelity. So will eternal punishment for evildoers, whose bodies will be rejoined to their souls. Justin speaks of the power of the cross which Jesus took upon his shoulders[31] but he does not specify it beyond saying that "a crucified man who is First-begotten of the Unbegotten God will pass judgment on the whole human race."[32] In short, deliverance to a risen life of bodily incorruptibility for Justin, and its opposite shame and corruption, will follow upon the free choice of the teachings of Jesus or their rejection.

In this the *Apology* resembles the treatise known as *Second Clement*, sometimes called "the first Christian homily," which comes from the same period or earlier, probably written in Egypt. Its author promises entry into God's kingdom and repose there for those who keep their baptism pure by guarding the flesh as God's temple. "If Christ the Lord who saved us was made flesh though he was at first spirit, and called us in this way, in the same way we too in this very flesh will receive our reward."[33] *Second Clement* has retained more elements of New Testament apocalyptic than most of the second-century writings. "Loving and doing what is right," its author says, "we must be on the watch for God's kingdom hour by hour, since we do not know the day when God will appear."[34] Quoting from Isaiah 66:18 and 24, the author refers the vision of the gathering of the nations on Zion described there to the day of Jesus' appearing, "when he will come to redeem us, each according to his deeds, and [unbelievers] . . . will be surprised to see the sovereignty of the world given to Jesus."[35] But the chief mode of deliverance in this brief treatise is heartfelt

---

[30]*Ibid.* (10), p. 247.

[31]*Ibid.* (35), p. 264.

[32]*Ibid.* (53), p. 276.

[33]*Ibid.* "An Anonymous Sermon, Commonly Called Clement's Second Letter," ed. and tr. C.C. Richardson (9.5), p. 196.

[34]*Ibid.* (12.1), p. 197.

[35]*Ibid.* (17.4-5), pp. 200-01. Cf. 16.3, p. 200, which quotes Malachi 4:1 and Isaiah 34:4.

repentance for former sins whereby believers will be saved. Such repentance follows the sufferings Jesus Christ endured for us, but how is not specified. It will assure life in the kingdom for some and punishment, with torments and fire, for others who have done amiss and denied Jesus in word. Once again, the fact of a redeemed condition is made clear but it goes unaccompanied by any theological rationale.

St. Irenaeus of Lyons (ca. 180) has Christ Jesus coming from the heavens in the glory of the Father to restore all things, raising up the human race to execute righteous judgment on all.[36] In the creedal formula from which this statement is taken Irenaeus is entirely traditional. He explains the practice of certain gnostic sectarians who keep on "redeeming" the dying up to the moment of death by pouring oil or ointment mixed with water on their heads, providing a formula with which to challenge the Powers when they meet them after death. He exposes the dualistic salvation schemes of Cerdon and Marcion and contrasts these teachers unfavorably with the "barbarians in speech" he knows who, without benefit of written documents, have an undiluted faith in "old tradition" and who have salvation written in their hearts by the Spirit.[37] The closest Irenaeus comes to a theory of redemption occurs in Book V of what has been called "the first work of Christian theology." There he sets out in chapter 1 the traditional teaching on redemption by Christ's blood as a ransom for those led into captivity. Only from our Teacher, the Word made man, could we have learned these things, he says. Apostasy had tyrannized us and in an unnatural way alienated us who, by nature, belonged to God Almighty. God's Word [restored us], making us his own disciples.[38] This same Lord

> gave his soul for our souls, and his flesh for our bodies, and poured out the Spirit of the Father to bring about the union and communion of God and humanity—bringing God

---

[36] *Ibid.*, "Refutation" (I.10), p. 360.

[37] See *ibid.* (III.4.1-2), pp. 374-75.

[38] *Ibid.* (V.1), p. 385.

down to humans by [the working of] the Spirit, and again raising humanity to God by his incarnation—and by his coming, firmly and truly giving us incorruption . . .[39]

This exchange of deity and humanity destroys all the teachings of the heretics. As expressed by Irenaeus, however, it does not bring a redemptive theology notably beyond familiar creedal affirmations. That will come with his theory of "recapitulation," better translated "renewal (*anakephalaiōsis*)," in which the Lord by his obedience on the tree renewed what was done by disobedience in (connection with) a tree.[40] As Eve, committed to a man, was led by the word of a messenger to flee from God, having rebelled against God's word, so Mary betrothed to a man, by the word of a messenger received the glad tidings that she would bear God by obeying the Word.

> As the human race was subjected to death through a virgin, so was it saved by a virgin, and thus the disobedience of one virgin was precisely balanced by the obedience of another. Then indeed the sin of the first-formed man was amended by the chastisement of the First-begotten, the wisdom of the serpent was conquered by the simplicity of the dove, and the chains were broken by which we were in bondage to death.[41]

This may seem like no more than St. Paul's counterbalancing the reign of sin through the deed of one man with the grace of God and gracious gift of another: acquittal and life replacing condemnation and death (Romans 5:12-19). Irenaeus supplies Eve as Adam's companion in sin out of Genesis, Mary as Jesus' companion at the cross out of John. But he has done more than add two women to the Pauline figure. He has identified Christ as "a new source of higher life,

[39] *Ibid.*, p. 386.
[40] *Ibid.* (19), p. 389.
[41] *Ibid.*, p. 390.

overcoming the defects of a basically good yet weakened first creation.... The new life is primarily life in Christ, of whom Irenaeus anticipates an Alexandrian epigram when he says that he became what we are so that we might become what he is."[42] Divinity becomes humanity so that the human might become divine. A weakened human race has been replaced by another race which has as its strength the gift of the Spirit.

> The Lord declares himself to be the son of man, so renewing in himself that primal man from whom [human] formation by woman began, that as our race went down to death by a man who was conquered we might ascend again to life by a man who overcame; and as death won the palm of victory over us by a human being, so we might by a human being receive the palm of victory over death.[43]

Thus does Irenaeus conceive the renewal of humanity on a Pauline model. Like Paul he first acknowledges the ransom figure in which the human race is purchased by the blood of Christ, but like Paul he goes beyond it—not simply to a transfer of dominions but to an interiorly divinized humanity (see Galatians 2:20). The old Adam-sin-death human race is no more. The Christ-obedience-life human race has succeeded it. The Savior's work has been to bring humanity not simply into a new age but into a totally new state.

This brief examination of half the total of extant second-century Christian writing should convince us of the fragmentary nature of the evidence on the redemptive mystery. The authors were addressing themselves to those outside the faith, it should be remembered, chiefly pagans and gnostics. They introduced discussion of the Christian mysteries, not for reflection by believers but to show outsiders that the Christian teachings were neither absurd nor contradictory. Aside from the Psalter and other biblical prayers, we do not have the liturgical texts both fixed and spontaneous that formed them

---

[42]E.R. Hardy, "Introduction," in Richardson, p. 351.

[43]Irenaeus, *Refutation* (21), in Richardson, p. 391.

in faith on a regular basis. Justin in his *First Apology* does provide the shape of the Sunday Eucharist and Hippolytus' fullscale exemplar of the same (ca. 215 in Rome)—the first that we possess—comes remarkably close in fleshing out Justin's steps. But, apart from what *Second Clement* and the erratic ethical treatise *The Shepherd* of Hermas tell us, we do not know much of how second-century Christians spoke their faith among themselves.

The paucity of references to Paul's letters in comparison with the use of the sayings of Jesus—often in pre-gospel form—has caused some to say that Paul was "domesticated" early. He was portrayed as if an itinerant preacher of the forgiveness of sins and the resurrection of the dead in Acts, in this view, and thoroughly compromised by the attribution to him of the epistles to Timothy and Titus. But the apparent disregard of Paul's letters by all but Clement, the writer *To Diognetus*, and Irenaeus may be more attributable to the epistles' not having been collected and circulated until Marcion's challenge (ca. 175) than to any conspiracy to defuse the Pauling teaching. Very much in possession was the easily grasped sacrifice of Christ to which a repentance of sins in faith corresponded, as a way to explain their forgiveness. To this was coupled belief in a risen life of glory with Christ and a life of eternal shame for the impenitent—since Jewish eon-thought was fading fast— and the second-century picture of redemption was almost complete. Fragments of awareness of Paul's teaching on the restoration, and more, of pre-Adamic righteousness emerge but they are just that—fragments. Then Irenaeus, writing in Greek toward the end of the century, proposes a total renewal of our race in the image of Christ. As God's Logos, Christ was the exemplar and prototype of the image of God according to which humanity had been created. Assimilation to Christ or imitation of him had to be especially in the obedience of his passion, which on the tree of the cross undid the damage done by the tree of disobedience.[44]

Tertullian (d. ca. 225) writing in Latin was shortly to develop

---

[44]See *Refutation*, V.16.

in North Africa the concept of "satisfaction," a term he may have derived from Roman law. It was to be developed fully as a description of Christ's sacrificial death only in the Middle Ages. At law it meant personal indemnification or public punishment but as Tertullian used it the term described the reparation made necessary by sins after baptism. In the years when a formal penitential system was being developed, this legally-minded layman could write of God as "one to whom you may make satisfaction," although he never used the term "satisfaction" for the death of Christ.[45] "One who repented was 'making satisfaction to the Lord,' one who lapsed after repentance was 'making satisfaction to the devil'."[46] The furthest he went was to ask: "Who has ever redeemed the death of another by his own, except the Son of God alone?.... Indeed, it was for this purpose that he came—to die for sinners."[47] A century and a half later Hilary of Poitiers (d. 367) applied the term to the death of Christ, equating satisfaction with sacrifice and seeing in the cross Christ's reparation to God on behalf of sinners.[48]

When Christian writers employed the biblical term "ransom" as a figure for what the death of Christ achieved, they did not specify, any more than the Bible had, the one to whom the ransom was to be paid. It remained in the realm of metaphor. The Alexandrian scholar, Origen (d. in Palestine ca. 254) frequently spoke of Christ's being handed over by God to demonic powers, probably because of the prominence of demons in Christian thought as a force for evil. Origen looked upon the devil as the master of death and Jesus as turned over by God, first to him, then by the devil to those who were set against Jesus. In this conception, the human race was in the devil's possession until the ransom of the soul of Jesus was paid to him.[49] Such a line of thought prevailed until the late

---

[45]Pelikan, *op. cit.,* p. 147 quoting Tertullian *On Repentance* 7.14.

[46]*Ibid.,* 5.9.

[47]*Ibid.,* p. 148, *On Modesty,* 22.4.

[48]Hilary, *Exposition of the Psalms* 53:12-13.

[49]Origen, *Commentary on Matthew* 16.8; he identifies the deception as deliberately practiced on the devil, 13.9.

300s. It was developed by Gregory, bishop of Nyssa (d. ca. 395), in the form in which it reached the West. Humanity had placed itself in Satan's clutches by the fall, so he had a right to adequate compensation if he were to yield it up. When God offered him Jesus as a ransom he accepted, not recognizing the godhead concealed by Christ's human flesh. He could not hold Jesus once he had him but was himself caught, as a fish is by the hook which the bait has concealed.[50] "When he swallowed [the body of Jesus]," as Rufinus bishop of Aquileia (d. 410) develops the image, "he failed to notice the hook of Deity enclosed within it: so, when he swallowed it, he was immediately caught and, bursting the bars of the underworld, was dragged out from the abyss to become a bait for others."[51]

This theory first put forward by St. Basil's brother Gregory by no means represented the mainstream of fourth-century Greek soteriological thought. Gregory of Nyssa and Athanasius of Alexandria (d. 373) both viewed human restoration as achieved essentially by the incarnation. Athanasius in Platonic fashion saw all humanity as a unity and thought that the incarnation, in virtue of the divinizing effect communicated to human flesh, *was* in effect the redemption. He wrote: "Seeing that all were perishing as a result of Adam's transgression, [Christ's] flesh was saved and delivered before all others because it had become the body of the Word Himself, and henceforth we are saved, being of one body with Him in virtue of it."[52] In another place he narrows the scope of redemption by confining divinization to those who are in a special relation to the Word by intimate union with the Holy Spirit.[53] Gregory, similarly, could write that the Lord "conjoined himself with our nature in order that by its conjunction with the Godhead it might become divine, being exempted from death and

[50]Gregory of Nyssa, *Catechetical Oration* 22-24.

[51]Rufinus, *A Commentary on the Apostles' Creed* 16, tr. and annot. J.N.D. Kelly, "Ancient Christian Writers 20" (Westminster, MD: Newman, 1955), pp. 51, 119-20.

[52]Athanasius *Against the Arians* 2, 61 as quoted by J.N.D. Kelly, *Early Christian Doctrines*, 2d ed. (London: A. and C. Black, 1960), p. 379.

[53]Athanasius, *On the Incarnation* 27-32; Kelly, *loc. cit.*

rescued from the adverse tyranny. For his triumphal return from death inaugurated the triumphal return of the human race to life immortal."[54]

Both of these men found a place for the biblical notion of a sacrifice achieved in Christ's death. The language of Scripture was used, hence they appeared to be speaking of one victim substituted for another; but their teaching was more a matter of Christ's death and victory as, in effect, ours because of the union between his flesh and ours.[55] An important footnote to the conventional idea of ransom paid to the devil needs to be added. St. Gregory of Nazianz provides it. This Cappadocian father, unrelated to the brothers Basil and Gregory and the best theologian of the trio, faulted the image by calling it "shameful that that robber should receive ... a ransom consisting of God Himself, and that so extravagant a price should be paid to his tyranny before he could justly spare us."[56] Christ's blood was not a ransom paid to God the Father either, said Gregory of Nazianz, because it was unthinkable that the Father should have derived pleasure from the blood of the only Son. This was a genuinely important observation. All theories of redemption centering on Jesus' blood are hampered by the specter of a God who takes delight in the brutal death of an innocent young man—or even accepts it. Whatever the reason, Christians have never been sufficiently sensitive to this problem. Nazianzus avoided any hint of a satisfaction achieved on Calvary by saying that the Father accepted the lifeblood of Jesus because "it was fitting that sanctification should be restored to human nature through the humanity which God had assumed. As for the Devil, he was vanquished by force."[57]

It can be seen from the variety of opinions above that there was no single, clear theory in the patristic era of how human

---

[54]Gregory of Nyssa, *op. cit.*, 25 in Kelly's translation, pp. 381-82.

[55]See Athanasius *On the Incarnation* 20; Gregory, *Discourse against Apollinaris* 16; 21.

[56]Gregory of Nazianz, *Orations* 45, 22 as quoted by Kelly, p. 383.

[57]Kelly, pp. 383-84.

redemption was accomplished. Not until Anselm's *Why God Became Man* (ca. 1097) did rival parties hotly argue the question as they did the incarnation in the fourth and fifth centuries. As to what it consisted in, there was relative unanimity that it meant a human well-being in time and eternity that far outrun the gifts given at the dawn of humanity. Greek thought on salvation can be roughly divided into a "mystical unity" school which linked the redemption to the incarnation, beginning with Irenaeus' teaching on the renewal of the human race in Christ; a "ransom" school which at times took the form of a forfeit paid to the devil, viewing captive humanity as restored once the price of Christ's death was paid; and a "realist" school which pictured Jesus as substituting himself for a sinful race, reconciling it to God by paying the penalty justice required it to pay. All three theories and their tributaries had some biblical image or images as their starting point. Each also had a prevailing motif, either offended divine justice requited, or the restoration of immortality, or conquest of the devil by the innocent one in a contest of free wills which God permitted. Through it all, Christ's death, as the fully adequate sacrifice accepted by God for the remission of sins, not further examined but continually affirmed, ran like an unbroken stream.

Of the three models of salvation in Christ spoken of earlier, the teachings and example of Jesus and his passion and death have been developed fairly extensively. If the first brought revelation of the truth and the second forgiveness of sins and justification, his resurrection brought restoration to immortality and deification. That third emphasis was so pronounced in many Church fathers that it merited the title, the "classic" theory of the atonement. (That word atonement comes from "at one," the only contribution of the English tongue to theological discourse.) Christ as *nikē tō r*[*-ē s*], Lat. *victor*, was very important in Eastern expositions of salvation, viewed as the coming together of God and sinful humanity. The medieval Western emphasis on Jesus' sufferings preliminary to his death should not obscure the previous centrality in images of human redemption of him as glorious victor at the end. Christ was Adam's conqueror who by his resurrection won the victory over death for those who had been captive to it.[58] "He fought and was victorious ... by his obedience he utterly abolished disobedience. For he bound the strong man, liberated the weak, and by destroying sin endowed his creation with salvation."[59]

The ultimate victory of Christ described in 1 Corinthians 15:24-28 would bring all of God's creatures to a single consummation—in Origen's view, of even the Lord's enemies—until "the end has been restored to the beginning, and the termination of things compared with their commencement. . . . And when death shall no longer exist anywhere, nor the sting of death, nor any evil at all, then truly God will be all in all."[60] Canon 11 of II Constantinople (553) probably meant to anathematize any speculation of Origen which did not prove to be the Church's faith, like the restoration of all things in Christ (*apokatastasis pantōn*). He had entertained a theory of the preexistence and fallenness of souls and the continuing pedagogy of wicked humans, even the devils of hell, until evil should be no more. Such "universalism" has never proved popular, either because it seems to read too much into 1 Corinthians 15:28 or to stress the divine goodness that the divine justice is set at nought. Still, Gregory of Nyssa could teach without contradiction a non-static paradise in which one is never sated in looking on the blessed vision of God.[61]

Salvation was usually defined by the second-century apologists as revelation. It was referred to in the first three centuries as forgiveness, but always linked to salvation from death and the gift of everlasting life. Jews of the Pharisee persuasion would not have to be told about the hope of a risen life in the body but the argument was always made to pagans that, for believers, an immortal life lay in store. In the early centuries this hope was tied to the speedy return of Christ. Cyprian,

---

[58]See Irenaeus, *Refutation* 5.21.1-2.

[59]*Ibid.*, 3.18.6. For the "descent into hell" as a creedal phrase see Pelikan, pp. 150-51; J.N.D. Kelly, *Early Christian Creeds* (London: Longmans, 1950), pp. 378-83.

[60]Origen, *On First Principles* 3.6.3.

[61]Gregory of Nyssa, *Life of Moses* 2.

bishop of Carthage (d. 258), who was a disciple of Tertullian, added to the futurity of the hope by writing, like his teacher and like the evangelist John, that salvation from death was a matter of here as well as hereafter, since Christ, "who once conquered death for us, is continually conquering it in us."[62] The Christ who saved from death saved equally from sin. God alone could forgive sins, as the gospel said (Mark 2:7), so when Jesus forgave sins and restored to health—*sōtēria*, later *salus*, meaning the well-being of both the body and the soul—he proved that he was the Logos of God. The salvation he came to bring was a wholeness in both soul and body which manifested him as "Savior." It can almost be said that any healing of the human condition taken singly, or all taken together, in present or in future, qualified in the early Church as salvation.

We repeat, salvation was not theorized on at length if at all. It was simply presented as God's work in Christ on humanity's behalf through the powerful action of the Spirit. If accepted in faith it would ameliorate the human estate both in present reality and in hope. The painful limits imposed by hereditary sin could be removed in the present life, all except disease and death. Alienation from God and from fellow humans was at an end. The consequences of sin might recur if they were readmitted, but their root cause, death, was in for certain defeat in the future. This life of the redeemed who hoped for final salvation was never described as a present paradise. It was presented as a taste of what life had been like before human rebellion and would be again in its fullness for those who obeyed God in the manner of Jesus Christ. The practical consequence of this condition was to the fore in everyday living. The needs of the poor were met by the community. Persons were respected despite their social status. A support network surrounded individuals and families, making possible fidelity in chastity and charity in a way none had thought possible. At the heart of it all was the weekly Eucharist with Christ present among them in word and sacrament as a bishop

---

[62]Cyprian, *Epistles* 10.3; cf. Tertullian *Against Marcion* 1.24.7.

presided. The picture is not falsely idealized. It can be seen as true if one takes into account how small-scale the Christian reality was in every city and town, and how much impetus was provided by its counter-cultural character. Immense changes would come with the Constantinian settlement of 313 and even larger ones with the admission of the northern tribes after 600. But in the half a millennium after the apostolic age, despite chicanery of every sort in imperial and episcopal residences, redemption was a lived reality not crying out to be defined. Its center of gravity was in the life to come because of the hardships of the present age. It was, nonetheless, a reality of the here and the now.

One aspect of the life of the redeemed has not been touched on and must be. It is the Greek tradition of referring to the change effected in those reconciled in Christ as *theōsis*, divinization. This usage occurred especially in the mystical strain represented by men like Clement of Alexandria (d. ca. 215). It derived ultimately from 2 Peter 1:4 which spoke of "sharers of the divine nature." The final settlement of the struggle over the divinity of Christ would be required to distinguish between his status as the incarnate Logos and the way the Christian in grace participates in the mystery of godhead enfleshed. Still, Clement's phrase, "the Logos of God became man so that you may learn from a man how a human being can become God"[63] has survived to this day, by way of an old Roman collect, in a prayer over the water to be mixed with wine in the eucharistic rite. Origen and Irenaeus likewise spoke of salvation as the attainment of the gift of divinity. Basil writing *On the Holy Spirit* (9:23) and Cyril *On the Trinity* (7) could both affirm that it is the Spirit that makes us God. Athanasius was to become the chief spokesman for the position that God the Word had become human so that human beings might become God.[64] "By the participation of the Spirit we are

---

[63]Clement of Alexandria, *Exhortation to the Greeks* (*Protreptikos*), 1.8.4. Cf. "By the mystery of this water and wine, may we come to share in the divinity of him who humbled himself to share in our humanity."

[64]Athanasius, *Against the Arians* 2.69-70.

knit into the Godhead."[65] So firmly entrenched was this conviction that in the christological debates of the fourth and fifth centuries the proponents of the union of the two natures in Christ in one divine person used the argument that divinized humanity—which was assumed as a fact—could only have been achieved by a Logos united with human nature.

Maximus the Confessor (d. 662), who is acknowledged as the father of Byzantine theology, took the idea of salvation as deification from the earlier Greek fathers and developed it as the central biblical message.[66] This champion of orthodoxy had his tongue cut out and right hand cut off at age eighty-two by fellow Christians for his opposition to the monothelete heresy, small gestures which seem to negate anything that was said about the redeemed condition of believers in the pages above! These indignities were heaped on him after a lifetime of maintaining that being united with Christ was the means of deification. Similarity to Christ was a deifying force: that which made human beings divine.

The early medieval Symeon, the "New Theologian" (d. 1022), was a monk and mystic in the tradition of Origen and the seventh-century Syrian writer Dionysius the Areopagite. His prayer life, expressed in exhortations to fellow-monks, determined his theology. Every Christian and not monks alone, he wrote, had to become a "partaker of the divine nature" (2 Peter 1:4). "The resurrection of Christ is the same as our resurrection."[67] Assimilation to Christ was so intimate for every generation that all ages have the same relation to him as the apostles. It was not merely a union to be expected in heaven but something of now in this present life. Whoever was "single-minded" (Matthew 5:8) would see God already here and now. Gregory Palamas (d. 1359), another monk and mystic, was the systematizer of Symeon's teachings. As a theologian of ex-

[65] *Ibid.*, 3.24.

[66] For a summary of Maximos' teaching on salvation as deification, with extensive citations, see Pelikan, *op. cit.*, 2 *The Spirit of Eastern Christendom (600-1900)*, pp. 10-16; cf. Polycarp Sherwood, O.S.B., *The Earlier "Ambigua" of St. Maximus the Confessor and His Refutation of Origenism* (Rome: Gregorian University, 1955).

[67] Simeon, *Catechetical Sermons* 13, cited by Pelikan, p. 257.

perience he required believers to experience the things of the Spirit. They would thereby know the message of salvation to be the central element of the gospel. Palamas "interpreted salvation as immortality, as the gift of humanity, as the disclosure of authentic humanity, as purification, as the conjunction of the divine and the human, and above all as deification—patristic ideas all, but synthesized into what must be called a 'new theology'."[68]

[68]Pelikan, pp. 262-63.

4

The Medieval Debate
and the Watershed
the Reformation Constituted

In the Christian East, as the concluding pages of the last chapter pointed out, salvation had come to be viewed by the seventh century as deification. The supposition was that the early fathers had never taught anything else. Maximus the Confessor puzzled over the question of why this mystery of the church's faith was not included in the creeds with the other dogmas, but did not venture an answer. He and his generation were sure, relying on the teachings of Clement of Alexandria, Athanasius, and the Cappadocians joined by the neo-Platonist Syrian monk Dionysius, that true knowledge of God began with faith in the Scriptures as interpreted by the fathers who taught with one voice. This knowledge purified and illumined, preparing for birth from God. Such birth was adoption and gift, not anything that human beings could earn. It led to an eternal deification which would be marked by physical resurrection and incorruptibility.

There was no doubt in Byzantine theology that the human condition was one of sin, corruption and death. But the fundamental human problem was not sin, it was corruptibility. To overcome it, the process of deification had begun for all the baptized and not just those called to perfection. The Logos of God had become human in order to restore the human race to the godlike condition—that is, non-material, dispassionate—

in which it had been created. Reconciled humanity was on its way to a union with God not unlike that of the humanity of Jesus joined to the eternal Logos.

Maximus taught that by living as faithful Christians some rose from the flesh they shared with Christ, to his "soul"; by contemplation others proceeded from his soul to his "mind"; and a few moved on from the mind of Christ to his godhead. The monastic teacher had no illusions that great numbers would make this threefold progress. It was an ideal he held out, being careful to insist that true knowledge of God in Christ was the first rung on which all must stand. There is no way of knowing how many ordinary Christians from the rural peasantry or the cities were affected by his lofty teaching. We only know that the extant liturgies in which they prayed were in this spirit, and that in the tradition-bound East the sermons and treatises of the fathers were the pulpit fare of the people. Christian practice undoubtedly fell far short of the mystical ideal. It was, however, the ideal presented to simple folk and not just to a monastic elite. They never supposed themselves called to *be* God as Christ the Logos was. Deification did not mean that. Believers were sure only of this: that growth in intimate union with Christ would decrease in them the force of passion, the tendency to bodily corruption, and their sins, which threatened the adoption as children that God held out to them.

The Inevitability of Sin vs. Freedom Under Grace

In the East, in response to pagan convictions about fate and chance, human free will and responsibility were taught unequivocally. It was the gnostics who stressed the human incapacity to avoid sin and the entrapment in matter from which there had to be escape. As a result, Greek Christianity took human freedom for granted as it worked in conjunction with the grace of God that pervaded the cosmos. Pagan gnostics and Christian heretics were the opponents of such freedom. In the Byzantine orbit its existence never became the subject of theological debate. Whether the anxiety attributed to late antiquity in the West, as the fall of the empire came on (430-76), was the cause or the effect of the debate over liberty of choice may never be known. What is sure is the part played by the highly influential St. Augustine. His uncertainties about the capacity for freedom left by the ravages of primordial sin must have resonated widely in the culture, for single-handed he could never have convinced the West of its woundedness. In any event, the robustness of the Eastern conscience, convinced of its assimilation to godhead from the day of infant baptism onward, was not matched in the West. Latin Christianity came to doubt what humanity could achieve on its own were it not for supportive grace.

It is important to recall that when the British (Irish?) monk Pelagius first came to Rome he was scandalized by the laxity of Christian life there, and especially by the view that God's grace was solely responsible for human salvation. Humanity's part was thought to be correspondingly little, namely accepting under the impulse of grace that grace which God held out. Pelagius held the traditional position on the necessity of an ascetical life. Augustine was at first the innovator. It was Augustine who, by his writings, defined Pelagianism, a heretical position which Julian of Eclanum and Coelestius probably espoused and Pelagius, at least in the Augustinian form, did not.

Augustine had been influenced by Cyprian (*Letter* 64) to see in the necessity of infant baptism a proof of the inevitability of inherited sin, for which infants were in some sense responsible. It was Tertullian who taught him to recognize in Adam "the pioneer of our race and of our sin" (*Exhortation to Chastity*, 2.5). Augustine joined these considerations to Ambrose's teaching that Christ's virgin birth had kept him free of hereditary sin. Making a synthesis of the three elements, he deduced the doctrine of "original sin." St. Paul's epistle to the Romans provided him with the scriptural basis he needed. It taught that Adam's sin, literally understood, was so heinous that all humanity was originally and radically condemned for it: "And it cannot be pardoned and blotted out except through the one Mediator between God and humans, the man Jesus Christ, who alone could be born in such a way as not to need to be reborn. ["]1 This became the Western Church's prevailing reading of the mystery of human redemption. The legacy of sin could be removed only by faith in the one Mediator's effective intercession, achieved by his death on the cross. The Church never defined the sex act as the means of transmission of guilt. Augustine thought this to be the case because passion inevitably outran rational control. The Church said at the Council of Orange (529) only that both death and sin "passed" from Adam to all his progeny.[2] Most Western Christians probably think that Augustine's teaching on the passionate nature of sex as sin is the Church's teaching, so lengthy a shadow did this giant cast. They have also mastered his version of the Adam-Christ typology so thoroughly (which rendered the *aph'ho* of Romans 5:12 as *in quo*, "in whom"—Adam, understood—instead of the correct *quia*, "inasmuch as") that for fifteen centuries they have been convinced that St. Paul taught that all humanity was sinful in Adam's loins. In fact, Paul taught the primordial sin of Adam and all humanity following his lead, but not the hereditary "original sin" of Augustine.

The bishop of Hippo was so convinced of God's freedom to act without any external constraint, above all one imposed by free human creatures, that he accounted creation sheer grace and human righteousness the same. Grace alone could transform the human will, wounded as it was by Adam's sin, to render it capable of doing good. God's grace is sovereign because God's will is sovereign, a conviction Augustine derived from the Bible. His view of the unchangeable essence of God came from his neo-Platonism. The creation was flawed through and through by Adam's sin. Only the universal love and favor God bore it could restore its integrity. Augustine at first conceived God to be the foreknower of all that free angelic

---

[1]Augustine, *Enchiridion on Faith, Hope and Love*, 48. See a translation by Henry Paolucci (Chicago: Henry Regnery, 1961). Pelikan, *op. cit.* 1.278-331 provides all the pertinent citations from Augustine's works in his Chapter 6, "Nature and Grace."

[2]Council of Orange, canon 2, Denzinger-Schönmetzer, *Enchiridion Symbolorum*, 32d ed. (Freiburg: Herder, 1963), 372 [175], p. 132.

and human wills would choose. Later he came to think that the nature of deity demanded that God not only foreknow but also predestine all free choices. Grace was a gift that could not fail of its effect. Predestination was but the preparation for grace.

A double predestination to heaven and hell was, for Augustine, simply the omnipotence of God achieving its purpose. Facing the question of why an all-good God would freely predestine some creatures to hell, Augustine's answer was: to manifest the divine wrath and to demonstrate the divine power.[3] St. Paul's final soliloquy in Romans 11 (v. 33) was his response to the mysteriousness of it all. God's election was simply beyond his comprehension. So sure was Augustine of double predestination, however, that to the end he argued 1 Timothy 2:4, "God wishes all to be saved and come to a knowledge of the truth," to mean, "wishes all to be saved who would be saved." He was not followed by the Church in this interpretation of the passage, which it took to mean God's universal will to save.

The Augustinian Tradition Crystallized

Salvation for Augustine was ultimately the bestowal of divine grace, made available through the Church and its sacraments in such a way that all sins, original or actual, were removed. The gift of the Spirit was given, accomplishing a baptized person's rebirth. And if the grace of persevering to the end was accepted there was the lively hope of an unending life at death. Augustine was the author of as many and as beautiful homilies about new life in Christ on the occasion of Christian initiation as Cyril of Jerusalem, Chrysostom or Ambrose. More could not be asked from him. Yet he ultimately provided the West with a catechesis of an intellect darkened and a will weakened by the sin of Adam, the stain of original sin washed away by baptism, a prevenient and con-

[3] *A Literal Commentary on Genesis* 11.8.

current grace required for any "salutary" act, and a salvation from the pains of hell which meant at the same time the blessed vision of God. His *civitas dei* ("republic of God") was in fact the earthly assembly of those obedient to God who were mixed in with those resistant to God's will. The center of gravity of his "salvation," however, was the community of the blessed in heaven. Augustine undoubtedly believed in the deification of humanity as firmly as any Eastern father. What came through was a lifetime of hope that by cooperating with God's grace one should prove to be among the elect.

"Whoever (*Quicumque*) wishes to be saved," read the anonymous fifth- or sixth-century Athanasian creed, "must, above all else, hold the Catholic faith." This is defined as worship of the one God in trinity and trinity in unity, plus faithful belief in "the incarnation of our Lord Jesus Christ." The formulary was derived almost entirely from Augustine's treatise on the trinity but with the elimination of all begetting, proceeding or sending. Father, Son and Spirit were co-equal, co-eternal, co-everything-else one could say of God. Verbal acknowledgement of trinitarian faith was very much the path to salvation in the thousand years after Augustine, with the warning of the Athanasian Creed that "all would have to give an account of their works" never forgotten.

Augustine's great expositor who acted as a bridge to what would be termed the middle ages was Pope Gregory I ("the Great," d. 604). He was the custodian of the traditional Augustinian thought that would lead to scholasticism. Gregory never deserted the reinterpretation of the Greek fathers that Augustine provided, adding to it obedience to the Roman see as the touchstone of doctrinal orthodoxy. Although most of Gregory's material was from Augustine it was he who was the most widely read Western father in the middle ages. The expositors of Augustinian thought via Gregory were men like Bede and Alcuin in England, Boniface the apostle to the Germans, and Isidore, Leander and Ildefonse in Visigothic Spain. They defined salvation as a free gift of unmerited grace and taught that the way to it was keeping the commandments, seeing no contradiction between the two. The law of Christ had to be obeyed if people were to be with him in the future life.

Yet Augustine's teaching on the necessity of grace at all points of human action was never deserted. One sinned by human power alone. Grace was needed for a return to the right path. Without grace no one was capable of anything good. In expounding the tension between faith and good works, a tension represented by Paul to the Romans and the epistle of James, these pre-medieval teachers sought compromise. It was grace that achieved anything good in human choice, even the expression of that gift which was good works. The missionary preaching of those busy centuries, the seventh through the ninth, presented Christ the preacher who died and rose as a person to be imitated, his commandments kept, and the word and sacraments of his Church availed of, if anyone hoped to be saved. The teachers of that age insisted that the sufferings of Christ invested the sacraments with power. They speculated on the afterlife, specifically whether the apostles, the martyrs and the perfect enjoyed the blessed vision of God immediately at death. They also came to the consensus position on purgatory which Augustine had proposed speculatively and Gregory solidified,[4] holding this intermediate state to be defined by the statements of "many of the fathers" in extension of passages like Matthew 12:32 and 1 Corinthians 3:12-15.

If anyone asks how the teaching of Scripture fitted into all this, the answer is that it was intertwined in every sermon, treatise, and catechical lecture. There was, besides, extensive exegesis of the books of the Bible. Whatever the literary medium, the framework was always the Church's teaching as it was enshrined in the creeds, the councils and the fathers. There was no such thing as the use of the Bible which Protestant Christians might expect, namely the uncomplicated presentation of a number of passages from the gospels, St. Paul and other biblical places to establish the faith of the Church concerning the mystery of redemption. That approach to the Bible was not to be devised for eight hundred years. The Catholic (later in the east called Orthodox) tradition was, above all, a tradition: that which was handed on. Nothing in

---

[4]Augustine, *The City of God* 21.13, 23-24; Gregory the Great, *Dialogues* 4.29.

this rich tapestry was ever lost. If there was a change of emphasis or an addition or deletion it was not identified as a change but as what was always present in the apostolic teaching, best testified to by the Scriptures. New applications and new emphases were constantly being discovered but never new teaching; that was called heresy. "There could not be opposition between Paul and other apostles, for there could not be any opposition in Scripture anywhere."[5] All tensions and contradictions were resolved. All new developments were identified as having been there in the original deposit.

Some Early Medieval Debates

By the seventh century, Isidore, archbishop of Seville (d. 636), was able to describe the present, mortal life as unimportant in its duration next to "that life for whose sake you are a Christian, namely life eternal ... , the vital life."[6] As the pagans came streaming into a Church that was fast becoming identified with the culture, salvation was increasingly being proposed as life in the kingdom of the future, the heavenly homeland.

A ninth-century dispute between Hincmar archbishop of Reims (d.882) and Gottschalk a monk of Orbais (d. 868), on the triune nature of God and "adoption" as a term proper to the humanity of Christ, brought out the necessity of incorporating theologically the *person* of Christ into the *work* of Christ. A formal consideration of how his human nature functioned to redeem the human race was long overdue. The role Mary played in the redemption achieved by her Son had begun to be raised by the monks Bede (d. 735), Ambrose Autpert (d. 784) and Paschasius Radbertus (d. 865). To crown it all, Hincmar and Gottschalk locked horns over Augustine's double predestination, the former denying that it was part of the Catholic faith and the latter defending it as such. No one

---

[5]Pelikan, *op. cit.*, "3 The Growth of Medieval Theology (600-1300)," 1978, p. 41.

[6]Isidore of Seville, *Opinions and Conclusions (Sententiarum)*, 3.61.5.

could question that Augustine taught it, while the Council of Orange omitted mention of it.[7] Gottschalk thought that there was no such thing as free will without grace, Hincmar that the will was rendered non-responsive and weak but not dead by Adam's fall. Both claimed Augustine as their authority but neither wished to say that, for Augustine, God thoroughly determined all good and evil. Matters were advanced by the claim of John the Irishman (Scotus Erigena, d. ca. 877), a disciple of Maximus who knew Greek as few Latin-speakers of this period did, that dialectics were part of revelation. This made the dialectical process a source of knowledge of divine things—a position to be revived by logicians of the twelfth century such as Abelard. The 900s saw little or no progress in theology but they did witness the spread of Benedictine monachism. In the social setting of monasteries on the land surrounded by agricultural communities of peace, a European peasantry experienced something of salvation as total human well-being. Abuses such as abbots acting as huge landholders had not yet crept in. A measure of the order and harmony that presaged the rule of God proclaimed by Jesus became available in isolated parts of Europe and the British Isles.

Peter Damiani, an Italian monk and later cardinal (d. 1072), was the forerunner of a series of disciples of Anselm who tried to bring the person and work of Christ together on a doctrinal basis. They spoke of a "plan" of salvation, with *ordo salutis* doing the work of *oikonomia* in Ephesians 1:10 and *prothesis*, "purpose", one verse later (cf. also 3:11). In this plan the life, death and resurrection of Christ were seen as divinely ordained events calculated to achieve human restoration from its weakened condition. The incarnation of the Lord was central in this work of God.

The Anselmian Theory of Redemption

St. Anselm of Bec (d. 1109) was born in northwestern Italy

---

[7]See Augustine, *Enchiridion* 26; 100.

but entered a monastery in Normandy. He would serve as archbishop of Canterbury for sixteen years, six of them in enforced exile. He wrote *Why God Became Man* as a meditation on the paradox of God's mercy and God's justice: the gift of reconciliation of the world to God, so undeserved (see 2 Corinthians 5:19), paired with the work of suffering and death so alien to God but apparently necessary to bring it about.[8] Anselm's *Cur Deus Homo* in part responded to the apologetic need of formulating intelligibly the doctrine of redemption at a time when Jews and Muslims were finding faith in a "crucified God" absurd. Anselm was not only a man who sang the office daily in choir. He was also a dialectician. In this treatise he tried to plumb the "necessary reasons" for the incarnation, "setting Christ aside as if nothing were known of him."[9] Anselm's rationalism is a theological one. Faith is its starting point, seeking understanding by way of argumentation and proof. He assumes as axiomatic the truth of creation, eternal life, and original sin in a way the modern age could not. Given his premises, the argument is ingenious. He thought that it demonstrated, i.e., proved his thesis.

Just as with Anselm's proof of the existence of God in the *Proslogion*, many first hear his theory of redemption in garbled versions. They come upon impatient dismissals without encountering any unbiased report of it, much less the argument itself. The chief misrepresentations declare it a dubious commercial transaction in which God accepts payment to himself, or else a requital of wounded honor such as a feudal lord might demand. Other versions see in it elements of placating an angry God or the mechanical substitution of Christ as the victim whem sinful humanity is the one rightly condemned. Before attempting to present what has been called Anselm's "theological masterpiece," we should acknowledge that it lay open to all the distortions it received once certain eleventh-

---

[8] Anselm, "Why God Became Man" in *A Scholastic Miscellany. Anselm to Ockham*, ed. Eugene R. Fairweather, X The Library of Christian Classics (New York: Macmillan, 1970), pp. 100-83.

[9] *Ibid.*, "Preface," p. 100.

century axioms of faith could no longer be taken for granted. It presupposed that something was known of the nature of God; likewise that the human plight was widely realized, a race Anselm described as "altogether ruined."[10] The theory further took for granted God's overcoming of sin and death on humanity's behalf—Christ the victor and the Holy Spirit the continuing guarantor of the victory, in the life of the Church.

Assuming all this, Anselm set himself to show *how* humanity's release from sin and death was accomplished. He mentioned at the start that he would write as if nothing were known of Christ, feeling confident he could prove that only a God-man who accomplished what Christ did could be the missing piece in the puzzle. The question that unbelievers scoffed at, and many of the faithful pondered, was why an incarnation and death were necessary for the life of the world when God could have achieved reconciliation through any other person, angelic or human, or even by a sheer act of will.[11] Anselm's problem was to provide "necessary reasons" why, given the nature of God and the straits in which humanity found itself, the dilemma could not be solved in any other way.

The monastic author tells his readers that he had to finish in Capua a treatise he began in Canterbury, a piece of remarkable restraint given his political troubles over lay investiture with England's king. He adopted the question and answer form as he had in earlier writings, once more in dialogue with his monastery confrere Boso. Knowing he could count on a knowledge of the fathers as they wrote of release from slavery to sin and death in the biblical imagery of sacrifice, he could also assume familiarity with the epistle to the Hebrews. There, Christ is a high priest of a human nature like ours who offered the one acceptable sacrifice for sin. Anselm operated in the classical mold by featuring God's initiative and power toward humanity, to which was inseparably joined a Godward human

[10] *Ibid.*, I.1., p. 101.

[11] *Ibid.*, I.4.A, p. 105.

response. He undoubtedly knew all about deification and a ransom from sin, whether paid to Satan or God or no one.

Disregarding all these, he starts with the divine honor (or majesty or essence) to which, after primordial sin has been committed, satisfaction must be paid. Why does he think that reparation must be made to God's glory? Is deity so fragile or so vain that every slight, great or small, must be rectified? Anselm would have thought that an unworthy conception of godhead indeed, scorning any who held it, even as legions have scorned him—who did not hold it. The divine glory or greatness is simply godhead. It cannot be added to or detracted from. "Injury" to God's feelings is inconceivable. But, given the acknowledgement of God that is necessary in the intelligent creatures God has made, cosmic balance must be restored if it is lacking from any quarter. Anselm thought it needless to say that only God could restore it. This is the "satisfaction" Anselm speaks of, literally "doing enough." It is neither payment nor repayment. While spoken of in terms of the honor due, it is actually the correction of an omission.

But, says Anselm, the offense in question is nothing like one that a person might visit on another. God is infinitely beyond the creaturely condition. This God than whom nothing greater can be thought can only be rendered an offense than which no greater can be thought. The slightest sin will do this because of the infinity of the subject offended. God being God, it cannot be otherwise. To such a one only infinite satisfaction can be made.

If all this sounds like life in a very large claims court, all such images must immediately be banished. One must think only of a God who creates angels and humans who *can* sin, faced with what to do when they *do* sin. The first thing that occurs to us, given our conception of the divine nature, is for God to dismiss all charges. At this solution the man of Canterbury would doubtless remind us how little we know about God. That answer to the problem certainly befits the divine mercy but there is such a thing as the divine justice. Again here, there must be no thought of a neighbor looking for damages or a nation seeking reparations. A God of justice is the only way godhead can be. Deity may be merciful without limit but it must at the very least be just—giving to creatures what is due them in light of the nature decided on for each; expecting likewise from each a fitting response according to its nature. A poet once of the Company of Jesus wrote:

> Snails do the holy
> Will of God slowly,

and another,

> the just man justices;
> Keeps grace: that keeps all his going graces;
> Acts in God's eyes what in God's eyes he is.

God cannot but be busy about the business of Godding. We call what requires this God's justice.

The other element in the equation is that the detractor from the divine glory is creaturely: all humanity in solidarity with its progenitor Adam. It could not be God who offended God. That is absurd. It is a finite being who has brought about an infinite offense. But, if it is true that the recipient of the offense determines the guilt of the offense, why cannot a finite being make infinite satisfaction? The answer is that when a human being or the whole race is obedient or repentant, or gives God glory in any way, that glory is finite because it is the acknowledgement of God's infinity proper to finitude. The cosmic balance is merely observed. When, however, Adam or the whole human race sins, the infinite God is denied the glory that should come from the creature. The offense is called infinite because something is lacking, so to say, on God's side. Hence only the action of God Infinite can restore the balance.

At the same time there must be a human reconciler because there was a human offender. This leaves the necessity of human salvation initiated and carried through at all points by God, yet at the same time a thoroughly human work. For this to be the case *Deus-homo* must be the actor, a God who is human without any compromise of deity or humanity. The incarnation is thus a necessity, given the problem to be solved in a way that does not diminish divine justice (glory, essence) or minimize free human responsibility. None of this, it should be needless to add, makes sense apart from the conviction of a humanity acting in solidarity of satisfaction as it did in solidarity of sin. *Homo* is the whole human race everywhere. Adam and Christ at two sensitive points in time act representatively of the whole—one inescapably because of temporal priority, the other by divine calling and free response.

The unbelievers to whom *Cur Deus Homo* is primarily directed have this problem: "In what captivity . . . in what prison or in whose power were you held, from which God could not deliver you, without redeeming you by so many labors and in the end by his own blood? If . . . God . . . could not do all this by a simple command you . . . make him powerless,. . . . [12] What justice is there in giving up the most just man of all to death on behalf of a sinner?"[13] Anselm's partial answer is that the Father did not give up the innocent to death for the guilty, nor force him to die, nor allow him to be slain against his will. Jesus readily endured death to save humanity. What seems to have been a divine command was in fact not compulsion.[14] He died, "simply because he constantly upheld truth in justice, in life and in word." All rational creatures owe this to God. "Christ freely underwent death not by yielding up his life by an act of obedience, but on account of his obedience in maintaining justice, because he so steadfastly persevered in it that he brought death on himself."[15] This clarification has not survived the centuries as it deserves to. It could have saved endless confusion. There was no God who said to Jesus: "You must die. It will set things right. This is my implacable will." There was in Jesus only "a Man who owed obedience to God, a humanity that owed it to his divinity." As a matter of obeying God by persevering in truth and justice, he freely let death overtake him. Interpretations of the meaning of this death followed, from the first century to the eleventh.

[12] Anselm, *Cur Deus Homo* I.6; Fairweather, p. 106.

[13] *Ibid.*, ch. 8, p. 111.

[14] *Ibid.*

[15] *Ibid.*, ch. 9, pp. 112, 113.

They were not all equally complimentary to God.

Anselm says that the incarnation and the satisfaction made to God by the Word of God incarnate can be called "necessary" only if it is clear that God acts under no compulsion. "This necessity [in God] is nothing but his own changeless honor, which he has from himself and not from another, and on that account it is improper to call it necessity. Nevertheless, let us say that it is necessary, on account of his own changelessness, for God's goodness to complete what he undertook for humanity, even though the whole good that he does is of grace."[16] This passage is important (and will be developed in our final chapter) because of its serene understanding that creation and redemption are a single mystery, not two. God did nothing to rectify what had gone awry in the work of creation. The work of God outside divinity is multiple in its effect but single in its cause which is deity itself (goodness, changeless honor). All that God does on humanity's behalf is graciousness: creation, redemption, sanctification. We humans deal with it as threefold and successive so as to get a handle on it. We attribute this threefold work of God—the terminology is ours—to God (Father), Word (Son) and (Holy) Spirit, as if each were in charge of one work. Anselm says correctly that the changlessness of God required that God's goodness complete what he undertook for the human race. (The Latin tongue, incidentally, requires no nominative pronoun of any gender for God, and *homo* describes a human being of either sex or the race collectively.)

There is a hint of the argument of the earlier *Proslogion* when Anselm says that whoever pays God for human sin must give something greater than anything that exists except God. "But there is nothing above everything that is not God, save God himself.... So no one but God can make this satisfaction." That occurs in chapter 6 of Book II. The basic argument of the dialogue is to be found immediately after it:

> *Anselm*: But no one ought to make [satisfaction] except a human; otherwise humanity does not make satisfaction.

---

[16]*Ibid.*, II, 6, p. 150.

Boso: Nothing seems more just.

A.: If then, as is certain, that celestial city must be completed [after the fall of the angels] by human beings, and this cannot happen unless the aforesaid satisfaction is made, while no one save God can make it and no one save a human *ought to* make it, it is necessary for a God-Man to make it.

B.: "Blessed be God!" We have already found out one great truth about the object of our inquiry."[17]

The argument proceeds from there to a review of Chalcedonian christology, showing why the desired effect could not be achieved if the Nestorian or Eutychean position were true (without naming either the council or the heresies): "Therefore, for the God-Man to do this, the person who is to make this satisfaction must be both perfect God and perfect man, because none but true God can make it, and none but true man owes it."[18]

The present writer has a vivid memory of a theological seminary in which two sermons were preached at every noonday meal throughout a semester by upperclassmen who were studying the tract *De Verbo Incarnato*. As preaching it was desperately bad. As theology it was much better than this twenty-year old took it for. He did not know he was getting straight Anselmian doctrine via a German theologian named Pesch. Being a youthful idealist he thought it mechanical, contrived, and, as he would have said pedantically, aprioristic. A little wisdom has intervened in the time between. To begin with, Anselm does not start with the fact of the incarnation as he seems to and then argue to its necessity. He begins by making the case for its necessity and concludes that it must have been the fact. More importantly, despite his unfortunate vocabulary of "satisfaction" (taken from Tertullian), "necessity," "owing" and "honor," he is not talking about a trans-

[17] *Ibid.*
[18] *Ibid.*, II, 7, p. 152.

action at all. Careful scrutiny reveals that the Anselmian argument is about one thing. That is that God, being God, can only act in God's way. Having decided to create us as free creatures out of love, God has to pursue us with this love no matter how we act. Once we chose to disobey and act sinfully— an almost incredible act of confidence in our freedom on God's part—the only path that God could follow was one of love for us in these tragic circumstances. The sole restraint imposed—if that is the correct term—is that God cannot act un-Godlike. Deserting the divine justice, necessity, call it what you will, would constitute such impossibility. Hence, there was the "need" to act as God did, becoming man and dying to show the extent of the love God bears us.

The argument Anselm mounted does sound at many points contrived, there is no escaping it. He *did* have Christ at the back of his thoughts all the time, despite his protest that he intended to argue "*Christo remoto*," i.e., setting him aside. But Anselm wished to get across to those who believed in neither incarnation nor redemption that Christians were not committed to an absurdity. That is why he attempted his philosophical approach, employing only such ideas about God and human nature as he knew Jews and Muslims held. If God is as the medieval world knew God to be, and if human sin is the tragedy it thought it to be, he argued, the love of God to achieve reconciliation with a repentant, free creature could take only one form: a show of total obedience by a human creature with nothing held back, by a person who is at the same time the God who alone can initiate such reconciliation. This medieval monk held fast to the basic fact which, if *it* is an absurdity, makes Christian faith absurd: God loves us to the point of dying a shameful death as one of us. Anselm thought this both possible and necessary and tried to prove it.

> Is it not right for him [*homo*] who, by his sin, stole himself from God as completely as possible, to make satisfaction by giving himself to God as fully as he can?.... But nothing that man can suffer for God's honor, freely and not as an obligation, is more bitter or harder than death. Nor can anyone give himself more fully to God than when he sur-

renders himself to death for God's honor. . . . [And] how could [the one we are seeking] give himself as an example to the weak and mortal, to teach them not to draw back from justice on account of injuries or insults or sufferings or death, if they did not recognize that he himself felt all these things?[19]

The Later Medieval Period: The Cross

It is not easy to deduce from the foregoing how constant in medieval thought was the theme of the all-pervasiveness of grace. Even the term "necessity" could be a synonym for grace and mercy in Anselm, while salvation was spoken of by other less well-known authors as accomplished by the grace or kindness of God alone. Some of this writing could give the impression that free will does not contribute anything to salvation but only grace. To this Anselm responded, in a treatise on grace and freedom, that the natural free will always assists the gift of divine grace.[20] The age was marked by many discussions of how the two worked in relation. A consensus position was that all human good was inspired by grace, which also conferred on free will the capacity to do good; yet while nothing good can be accomplished apart from the grace of God, no one should suppose that he or she could be saved regardless of effort.

The age was unquestionably one of Christocentric piety. Preachers and teachers reveled in the paradox of a God who had become our brother, a female creature who had given birth to her Creator, a babe lying in a crib who sent a star from the constellations to guide the magi. Peter Abelard (d. 1142), who was younger than Anselm by almost fifty years, could remark that while his period attempted to deal with the question of "what that redemption of ours through the death of Christ may be and in what the apostle declares that we are

[19] *Ibid.*, II, 11, p. 161.
[20] *On the Harmony* (*Concordia*) . . . *of the Grace of God and Free Will* 3.3, 4.

justified by his blood," Christians could count on the inherited belief of the age concerning what God was like and human nature and, among themselves, the incarnation.[21] Thus, even though no dogma of the atonement was ever defined, all the theories put forward about how it functioned took these three major realities into account.

The one matter that the present age finds egregiously missing in medieval discussions of redemption is human social well-being on this side of the grave as an essential component of it. Christ's conquest of the devil was featured, to be sure. Despite a firm belief in it, wars, disease and the grinding poverty of serfdom were such a daily reality that it was supposed that only individual deeds of charity could cope with their effects. A social response to social ills on any scale larger than a fiefdom (and many "kingdoms" were no more than that) was scarcely contemplated. The Jesus who had lived in the human community was the one whose example must be followed if anyone were to be led to salvation and blessedness. Often, because it was so hard to reform institutions, little came of the vocation to cooperate as a society in the world's redemption. But much came of individual conformity to Christ, which usually meant emulating his passion. To "bear the yoke of the cross" was to live a monk- or nun-like existence in the midst of the world. Abelard in the same chapter of his commentary on Romans quoted from above defined redemption as, "that supreme love [of God] in us through the passion of Christ." To believe in Christ's priesthood was to believe in him as savior and redeemer of the world, the one who opened to us the door to eternal life. He who taught righteousness infused it in us as an accompaniment of his love. It was not enough to imitate his example. Believers had to be participants of his merit, recipients of his grace.

The reconciliation or redemption of the world was so firmly fixed in the theological and the popular mind as having been achieved by the blood of the cross that anyone who featured availing oneself of its benefits by personal acts of emulation

[21] Peter Abelard, *Exposition of the Epistle to the Romans* 3

ran the risk of being accused of denying its objective character. By the plan of God and with the Spirit's cooperation, Christ had redeemed the world from sin and condemnation to hell by his voluntary dying. So firmly imprinted was this on the European consciousness that any other reading of the mystery— such as one that saw the resurrection as central—was imperiled. Some authors did identify the glorification of Christ as having an essential part in the plan of salvation, calling it a manifestation of him who had redeemed by his passion. If his life was a dayspring, the resurrection was the full light of dawn.[22] But the cross was redemption and redemption was the cross. St. Bernard of Clairvaux (d. 1153), writing *On the Love of God*, said that the effect of the redemption was that people had learned to love. But, for all classes and conditions of believers, it was the crucifixion that bodied forth God's love, revealing the will of God that they should love in return, even though they could not comprehend that mysterious will. The work of redemption was "the chief and the greatest of God's benefits."[23] The "self-emptying of God" (Philippians 2:7) made it possible to be filled with God, to be deified like the "deified man" which was the humanity of Christ.

In successive centuries, Odo of Cluny, Rupert of Deutz and Bernard of Clairvaux provided the sacred rhetoric that became the passion piety of the medieval Church. It went almost unchanged in the Reformation and modern periods. Bernard was clearly the most influential by both the bulk and the power of his writing. For him, constant meditation on the wounds of Christ was the refuge of the weak and weary. Glorying in the shame of the cross was the sure way to look forward to the glory of God. Paradise had been lost by Adam's sin but Christ the savior regained it. Bernard was insistent on a human response to God's love but, equally so, that the merits God required of believers had already been given them by prevenient grace. He accused Abelard of being overly

---

[22]Bernard of Clairvaux, *Exposition of the Song of Songs* 33.3.6.

[23]*Ibid.*, 11.2.3. Jean Gerson (d. 1429) and Nicholas of Cusa (d. 1464), both cardinals of the Roman Church and imaginative in their theology, could speak of salvation as deification, a participation in the power of God.

subjective in his approach to the mystery of redemption, a charge which Abelard's writings do not sustain. The so-called "subjectivity" of Bernard himself is well known but it is better described as affectivity or, in Wesley's later phrase, "warm-hearted piety." He certainly never lost sight of God as the justifier of the human race, not humanity the justifier of itself by its merits. "The righteousness of God," he wrote, "consists of his not sinning, but the righteousness of humanity consists in its being forgiven by God."[24] And with equal epigrammatic force, in another place, in response to the question of the part free will played in salvation: "It is saved. Take away free will, and there is nothing that needs saving; take away grace, and there is no way to save it."[25]

Bernard would be quoted copiously by both sides in the various Reformation controversies. Along with Augustine and Francis of Assisi of a century later he remains in the restricted company of Protestant saints. His teaching on grace and salvation was unequivocally Catholic but in the medieval manner. Relative to the texts of the liturgy and the writings of the patristic era, he would have to be called subjective. Such was the spirit of the age. The outlook on grace and salvation of most Western Catholics and all Protestants is distinctly Bernardian, whether consciously or not. Pre-Vatican II religious writing and prayer forms are almost all in that mold. The austerity of the liturgical movement which has its roots early in this century—a return to the Bible and the fathers as its sources—is not much to the taste of present sentiment. Bernard presents the paradox of the mailed fist of biblical piety in the velvet glove of sentiment (never quite sentimentality). It is hard to say which is the more authentic Bernard, but not hard to say which is the more attractive.

The Augustinian era had witnessed struggles on the sacraments as means of grace long before systematic attention was paid to how the grace of redemption operated. In that age Augustine prevailed over Cyprian with his view—which

---

[24] *Idem, Song of Songs* 23.6.15.
[25] *Idem, On Grace and Free Will* 1.2.

became that of the Church—that since Christ was the chief minister of the sacraments no unworthy minister could interfere with their grace effect if they were performed as the Church intended. The symbolic celebration once "done" (*opus operatum*), the saving grace of Christ became the possession of the Christian (called an *operans*) whose good disposition to receive this grace placed no obstacle (*obex*) of sin. Certainly popular religion with its almost boundless capacity for error could have thought of the sacraments as infallible producers of grace apart from human disposition. Still, there are enough sermons and popular literature extant to show the horror in which sacrilegious reception of the sacraments, especially the Eucharist, was held. These symbolic acts were the channels of divine favor which flowed freely if human resistance was not at work. Variously reckoned as between two and twelve in number, they were put at seven by the anonymous author of *Sentences of Divinity* ca. 1145, five of which all Christians receive and two, matrimony and orders, some receive. Peter the Lombard (d. 1160) incorporated the present seven into his *Sentences* (4.2.1), distinguishing them as *sacramenta maiora* from the *minora* like monastic vows and blessed objects, later to be known as "sacramentals." The latter could be occasions of assisting ("actual") grace, while the seven major symbols were causes of the Christ-life itself ("elevating," "sanctifying" grace).

The Middle Ages witnessed the growth of devotion to Mary and the saints as intercessors with Christ, in good part because the anti-Arian reaction of the years 450-600 had left the Church with a Lord who was thought of far more as consubstantial with the Father than sole mediator of our salvation. The cult of the martyrs, the apostles among them, created the first choir of heavenly advocates. Mary as the new Eve in Irenaeus and before that in Justin and Tertullian was traced in Chapter 2 above. There, she and Eve fleshed out the Adam-Christ figure of St. Paul. Her appearance in the early creeds served as a guarantee of Jesus' complete human nature, even if his was an extraordinary conception. The first known prayer addressed to her is one that may have originated in the third century. It was in Greek but is best known under its Latin title *Sub tuum praesidium*.[26] Four feasts commemorating her were developed in the East between the fifth century and the seventh, when the Syrian pope Sergius I (687-701) brought them to Rome: her divine maternity (visitation, presentation), annunciation, dormition, and nativity. In the middle ages devotion to Mary literally exploded, with cathedrals and shrines erected everywhere in her honor. She was widely hailed as a mediatrix with her Son through whose merits she too was saved, although whether from the moment of her conception was hotly disputed. From the twelfth century onward, iconography depicted her coronation in heaven at her Son's right hand. The cult of lesser saints proliferated in this period, so much so that Europe's peasants had an advocate with Christ for every trade and occupation. Awe before Christ's divine majesty was very much at work here, as if the *Deus-homo* who achieved our salvation could not be thought of as seeing to our safety.

The fourteenth and fifteenth centuries revealed every sort of doctrinal pluralism in Catholic Europe but, aside from some charges of heresy with resultant excommunications and executions, the fabric of the Church held reasonably firm. Some fissures like those of an ice floe showed themselves, but few could foresee the total break-up ahead. The Anselmian doctrine of redemption rooted in incarnation went largely unchallenged except by those of the Ockhamist-Scotist school who taught a will of God so sovereign that deity did nothing out of necessity. These voluntarists, who attacked the intellectualism of the Aristotelian scholastics, thought themselves the true inheritors of the Augustinian tradition. There was much apocalypticism abroad in those years. The anabaptist claim of the superiority of Spirit to structure was a rising tide. In general, a spiritualist strain was growing all over northern Europe which held Church leadership, priestly mediation and any material symbols of sanctification in increasingly lower esteem. The dereliction of pastoral duty by the clergy was certainly a factor here but the factors were many.

[26]Gerard S. Sloyan, "Marian Prayers" in J.B. Carol, *Mariology* 3 (Milwaukee: Bruce, 1961), 64-68.

Culture historians describe the age as anxious. They speak of the rise of the burgher class and the new learning and the wealth of the monasteries and prelates as doing much to bring on the cataclysm. Certainly all were contributory. It is doubtful, however, if anything more perceptive can be said than that the solicitude for their own souls' salvation of Luther and Calvin proved to be the spark in a variegated tinder box that waited to be ignited. There was, above all, a search for Christian perfection abroad at every level of society. The power of the Holy Spirit to work marvels in the human spirit was being discovered anew, almost as if it were nuclear energy eliminating the need for any lesser agency. There was at the same time a massive resentment of the social structures which gave political and religious power to a few and none to the masses. The powerless were a strange mixture of the learned, the rising middle class and the very poor. They seized on a power from which there was no appeal, the Spirit of God and the Word of God. Thus armed they would vanquish all their enemies real and imagined. There was at the same time an immense avarice at work in the human heart. The genuine religious reformers of the age were slow to learn the kind of volunteer army of God they had mustered.

The reformation era in and out of the Catholic Church defined the gospel as a message of salvation variously: the forgiveness of sins, the justification of the elect, the supremacy of the word and will of God over all human words and commands, salvation "by grace alone" with a consequent deemphasis on the power of the will, and the claim that one's eternal happiness is conditioned by the intensity of one's faith. These definitions of the gospel included some profound differences from what had gone before. They had to do with the practical apprehending of the merits of an all-sufficient death of Christ in satisfaction of the debt of sinful humanity. There was very little agreement, for example, on how the sovereignty of the divine will operated or on the measure of freedom the human will enjoyed apart from or under the impulse of grace.

The chief theological point at issue in the reformation was the nature of the Church. In what measure was it the custodian and interpreter of the gospel and how far was it under judgment of Scripture? The Lutheran doctrine of the all-sufficiency of justifying grace with its Augustinian anthropology could probably have been absorbed into Catholic theology if Luther at the high point of his career had ceased calling all the ordinances of the Christian religion except the proclamation of Scripture "Pelagian works." Compromise with the basic positions of Calvin on human depravity and double predestination would not have been so easy a matter. But since both held positions that had had a home in the Catholic Church of the previous two centuries, that is an untested proposition. The intent of both ultimately to break with the Roman Church as no longer the true Church is quite clear. It was chiefly in their ecclesiology, not in their view of how salvation was offered to the human race, that they differed from the Church they left. Agreement might even have been established on how the major Reformers and the Catholic Church viewed the way believers laid hold of "the benefits of Christ," in Philip Melanchthon's phrase (d. 1560). But the Church was the stumbling block. Defining it as an invisible congregation of the elect known to God alone had a Catholic history, if a fairly recent one. Defining it as an assembly of the justified who had no need of an ordained priesthood charged with dispensing the mysteries of Christ had none since the documents of the second century.

To read the canons of the Council of Trent on Adam's sin, its effect in us, and the remission of that guilt through the grace of Christ conferred in baptism is to be at home in the teachings of the Catholic centuries described in the chapters above.[27] Roughly the same things are said under Article Two of the Creed, "Of the Redemption," in Luther's *Short Catechism* of 1529[28] and the *Confession of Augsburg* (1530), with the difference that there concupiscence is equated with sin.[29] Articles IX-XI and XV-XVI of the Thirty Nine Articles of

---

[27]See Denzinger-Schönmetzer, *op. cit.*, 510-16 [787-92], pp. 366-68; cf. J.F. Clarkson, *et al.*, *The Church Teaches. Documents of the Church in English Translation* (St. Louis: B. Herder, 1955), 371-76, pp. 158-61.

[28]See Bettenson, *op. cit.*, p. 288.

[29]*Ibid.*, pp. 295.

the Church of England (1571) say substantially the same, including the statement that concupiscence "has the character of sin" (Art. IX.)[30] The major German, French and English Reformation documents differ from Trent and it from them in describing how believers avail themselves of the grace of redemption, but the differences are more apparent than real. This is a fact masked by the polemical rhetoric on both sides. The "faith" of the Reformers (*fides*; *fiducia*) has been shown by research to be the "hope" (*spes*) of Aquinas and the medievals, a firm trust that God will give to persevering believers all that the divine promises contain, including being with Christ in glory at the last.[31]

---

[30]See E.J. Bicknell, *A Theological Introduction to the Thirty-Nine Articles of the Church of England*; 2d rev. ed. H.J. Carpenter (London: Longmans, 1955).

[31]Stephanus Pfürtner, *Luther and Aquinas on Salvation*. Tr. by Edward Quinn. Foreword by Jaroslav Pelikan. New York: Sheed and Ward, 1964.

5

A Theology of Redemption
for Our Age

The struggles of the sixteenth century, as has been said, did not concentrate on how God saved the human race through Christ in the Spirit so much as on the anthropological question of how believers appropriated the merits Christ had earned for them. The Reformers, no less than the Catholics, were of the mind that Adam's sin was corporate in that its effects passed to all humanity. They had the warrant of Paul's letter to the Romans for that, and held to St. Augustine's view of original sin as hereditary guilt. But, because their theological bent was an extreme Augustinianism and hence pessimistic, they tended to think humanity severely wounded in all its faculties by this sin. The human race was so alienated from God that, of itself, it was incapable of doing anything good. The Catholics, influenced by their Dominican friar teacher Aquinas (d. 1274) and less by the Augustinian/Franciscan school which included men of the previous century like the theologian cardinals Gerson (d. 1429) and d'Ailly (d. 1420) and the Tübingen Professor Biel (d. 1495), were inclined to a more optimistic view.[1] They thought that rational creatures had been given control of their own destinies by God in the exercise of

---

[1] For a careful review of the early Dominican and the early and late Franciscan schools, the *via moderna*, and the medieval Augustinian school in these matters, see the Lutheran-inclining Alister E. McGrath, *Justitia Dei,* Vol. 1 (New York: Cambridge, 1986).

providence, of which the graced life of believers in Jesus Christ
was a part. One result was that sin did not invalidate "the
essential principles of nature" in them (the phrase is St.
Thomas's). This meant that a sinful human race could know
the dictates of natural reason even though it might be impaired
in fulfilling them. This Catholic commitment to a humanity
"deprived but not depraved" by Adam's sin—which was to
prevail at the Council of Trent—confirmed the Reformers'
worst suspicions that the Church they were breaking with was
given over to Pelagianism. They did not hesitate to say that it
was committed to creatures' saving themselves by their works,
not acknowledging righteousness as exclusively a divine quality.

   In their stress on the justification of the sinner by grace
through faith, the Reformers were perceived by the Catholics
to acknowledge insufficiently human freedom and the necessity
of good works. The Catholics, conversely, were totally committed, or so the Reformers thought, to salvation by works
apart from the grace of God because they lacked fiduciary,
i.e., trusting faith. In popular polemic neither side credited the
position of the other nor wished to, although at Trent some
like the general of the Augustinian Hermits Seripando (d.
1563) put the best case for the Lutheran position.

   Both sides held doggedly to the necessity of reliance on the
merits of Jesus Christ: since they had no merits of their own,
the Reformers said; since, as justified by God, they had been
made capable of meritorious action, the Catholics said. At the
base of the arguments about grace and merit was the
Reformers' contention that "the gospel" which served as the
norm and standard for every part of Scripture was the righteousness of God imputed to sinners who were justified "by
faith alone." This gospel of justification framed all other beliefs
and guiding practices of the Lutheran Reform. The Catholics,
on the basis of more centuries of history than the preceding
two, read the Scriptures and the fathers to say that there was
more to redemption than imputed righteousness. Thinking
erroneously, however, that a theology was being taught by the
Reform which set good works aside completely, they appeared
hesitant to acknowledge the fullness of the divine initiative and

continuing assistance, which had been at the heart of the Catholic tradition of East and West. It might be better to say that they continued to stress human freedom and responsibility as empowered by the grace of God, and were thought to be denying by that fact total reliance on God's justifying action.

Widespread Acceptance of the Anselmian Formulation

The debates of the sixteenth century on grace and free will, law and gospel are not directly the subject of this book. Its major concern is to explore how the Church believes God acts as humanity's savior, not how human beings receive and use the benefits of salvation. We shall later return to some of the major disputes on the mode of acceptance of the fruits of redemption, but only as it touches on the gift itself.

At the time of the gathering storm of the Reformation the Catholic West was at one in espousing St. Anselm's formulation of the doctrine of the atonement. His reading of the redemptive mystery could be called "definitive" in the late medieval period. Dante, Wycliffe, Hus, Thomas à Kempis, and Cardinal Nicholas of Cusa were among the cloud of witnesses to the doctrine that "no one could render satisfaction for the whole human race except God, and no one owed it to God except *homo*.[2] But while there was consensus that this formula accounted best for the demands of God's justice in tension with God's mercy, some in the fourteenth and fifteenth centuries modified the soteriology of the incarnation as a divine "necessity" (if, that is, God's honor were to be preserved) by stressing the primacy of the divine omnipotence and sovereign will. God willed freely whatever God wanted to will. Justice and mercy proceeded equally from this will. It governed all and was irrevocable. This view made the British Franciscan John Duns Scotus (d. 1308) say, in relativization of Anselm's

---

[2]Ubertino of Casale (d. ca. 1330) in *The Tree of the Crucified Life of Jesus* 1.7, 8, a Latin treatise ed. by Charles T. Davis, reprinted Torino, 1961. Some readers will recognize the name of the real life general of the Spiritual Franciscans from Umberto Eco's fictional *The Name of the Rose.*

position, that there was nothing necessary about Christ's death as the means of human redemption. It was strictly a matter of free divine foreordination. It could be called the "most fitting" means of redemption but it was not necessary; there were all sorts of means at God's disposal. The goodness of the incarnation and the cross was that God decided on this means to save.[3] A corollary of Scotus' position was that there could have been an incarnation by divine decree even if there had not been a fall, since the supreme work of God could not have been occasioned by any human event. The West followed Aquinas in that matter, who held the traditional position that God gave the gift of Christ to mend the damage caused by Adam's sin.

Martin Luther (d. 1546) was the heir of much of the Augustinian/Franciscan voluntarist strain in Catholic thought but it did not make him a Scotist on the doctrine of the atonement. It should first be noted that he was thoroughly Chalcedonian in his christology, although he would later be charged by Calvinists in debates on the eucharist with holding the Eutychean position. He expressed impatience with the speculations engaged in by scholastic theologians on the person and natures of Christ, saying that Jesus' selfhood was his own business while his, Luther's, concern was that this "Christ" was called such because he had acted as Savior and Redeemer for *him.* In general, the early German Reformers granted the correctness of Catholic teachers on christology but faulted them for their disregard of the primacy of soteriology. They accepted the Anselmian reading of Augustine and went immediately from there to a close examination of how the benefits Christ won were to be appropriated. Luther recorded in his *Smaller Catechism* (2.4) his belief that Christ, true God and true man, had redeemed him, "a lost and condemned creature, delivered me and freed me from all sins, from death and the

---

[3]John Duns Scotus, *Oxford Commentary on the Sentences* (*Opus Oxoniense*, available in Latin only), 3.19. q.un. 7; 4.4.7.4., Luke Wadding *et al.*, eds. *Opera Omnia*, reprint ed., 26 vols. Paris, 1891-95, as cited by Jaroslav Pelikan, *4. Reformation of Church and Dogma. 1300-1700* (Chicago: University of Chicago Press, 1984), pp. 26-27.

power of the devil, not with silver and gold but with his holy and precious blood and with his innocent sufferings and death, that I may be his, live under him in his kingdom and serve him in everlasting righteousness, innocence, and blessedness...." Clearly the emphasis is on what Christ achieved for the believer, expressed in terms of a lifetime of gospel liberty culminating in eternal happiness. The corresponding section of the *Large Catechism* (2.2.31) contained the Anselmian theory of satisfaction, one that Luther would espouse in his second set of lectures on Galatians in 1535 (there was a first in 1519). In this commentary he wrote that the Father gave instruction to the Son to "pay and make satisfaction for the sins of all" (on Galatians 3:13). Bugenhagen and Melanchthon, who are buried near Luther in the Wittenberg castle church, drew freely on Anselm's theory of satisfaction, saying that Christ chose to die freely in our place. Luther went beyond this common teaching of a totally adequate sacrifice that left nothing of our guilt or punishment to be expiated, writing for example in the Galatians lectures that the risen Christ was the absolute victor over sin, death and the devil. He quoted the Sequence of the eucharistic liturgy of Easter, *Victimae paschali laudes*:

> Mors et vita duello conflixere mirando:
> dux vitae mortuus regnat vivus,

which can be rendered:

> When in strange and awful strife
>   Met together death and life,
> He, once dead, but now the living
>   Leads to life and reigns, life-giving.

Luther was convinced that the scholastics had obscured this great central truth about Christ's victory. The divine and eternal person Christ, clothed as a sinner, had taken on himself the law and the curse of death and vanquished them utterly. Despite Luther's emphasis on the cross, he reckoned the life of Jesus into the cause of salvation more than Anselm had. He made Jesus an active fulfiller of the law, not just a passive victim of death, one who in his total obedience in life and death became for us our righteousness.

John Calvin (d. 1564) was thoroughly in the Catholic tradition in his views of redemption and reconciliation, adding as the third leg of his tripod, for special emphasis, election in Christ before the creation of the world. Between the first edition of his *Institutes of the Christian Religion* in 1536 and the last in 1559 he stressed increasingly double predestination and the reprobation of the damned. In the final edition he separated the providence of God from predestination, two concepts that he had long dealt with as one. He put pre-destination under the heading of appropriation of the grace of Christ through the action of the Spirit. Calvin attributed reprobation to a positive divine decree even more clearly than Augustine had, while claiming throughout that Augustine was supportive of his position. John Calvin's one notable departure from Anselm's theory of satisfaction was to insist that it was inadequate in its definition as the loss of righteousness. Adam by his sin had completely destroyed the image of God in which he had been created and replaced it by guilt, unrighteousness and unholiness. There is little in medieval Catholic writing to match the thoroughly depraved and loathesome creature that Calvin saw in humanity after the fall. At the same time, there are few who can match him for a conception of the awesome majesty of God and sovereignty of the divine will. Calvin wanted very much to be a herald of the love and tender mercy of God. The problem is that the grim logic of his premises (including the irrelevance of evil deeds to damnation!) terrifies everyone as much as he said the thought of hell terrified him.

The Catholic Response at Trent

When the Catholic Church in council finally faced the disciplinary changes needed to reverse several centuries of laxity, it decided it had to face the doctrinal challenge of the age as well. Meeting in the northern Italian cathedral town of Trento in twenty five sessions and with many interruptions (1545-63), it chose not to deal directly with the question of "justification through faith" ("alone," as Luther's addition to his translation of Romans 3:28 put it). It did issue a "decree" on original sin in an early Session—V in 1546—in which it said that Adam's sin consisted in the loss of "the holiness and righteousness in which he had been created."[4] This sin was then transmitted to the whole race "by propagation, not imitation."[5] The only *remedium* for it was "the merit of the one mediator, our Lord Jesus Christ, who reconciled us to God in his blood."[6] The first three of six anathemas of this session, with their quotations from the New Testament, should have had the acquiescence of the Reformers. Not so the fourth, which defended infant baptism against the anabaptists, while the fifth said that whatever had "the true and proper character of sin"—meaning not concupiscence or the inclination to sin—was removed rather than "smoothed over (*radi*) or not imputed."[7] Neither the anabaptists nor the Lutherans were named in the successive condemnations, only: "If anyone should say ... let him be anathema."

A decree on justification of Session VI early the next year said that "even though '[Christ] died for all' [2 Corinthians 5:15], still not all receive the benefit of his death, but only those with whom the benefit of his passion is shared."[8] This repudiates the teaching of both Augustine and Calvin that Christ died only for those who would be saved. There had been numerous disputes on this question in the late medieval period. Trent opted for the redemption of all humanity by God's intention, not just those who would in fact receive its ultimate fruits. The Decree of Justification of Session VI read in part: "God has set [Christ] forth as a propitiation by his blood through faith for our sins [Romans 3:25], not for our sins only, but also for those of the whole world [1 John 2:2]."[9]

---

[4] Denzinger-Schönmetzer, *op. cit.*, 1511 [788], p. 366.

[5] *Ibid.*, 1513 [790], p. 367.

[6] *Ibid.*

[7] *Ibid.*, 1514 [791], p. 367.

[8] *Ibid.*, 1523 [795], p. 369; Clarkson, *op. cit.*, p. 231.

[9] *Ibid.*, 1522 [794]; Clarkson *ibidem*.

The Decree on Justification came as the fruit of the first full year's work, appearing on January 13, 1547. It was a summary of centuries of biblical, patristic and theological teaching. No overt attention was paid in the sixteen "chapters" to the Reformers' peculiar emphases within that tradition, although they were very much in mind as the floor debates proceeded. Only when the Reformers were thought to have departed from it were their positions censured in thirty-three "canons" (an editorial distinction introduced by Seripando between Sessions V and VI of June and January). The redemptive theology of a transfer of kingdoms or allegiances featured by St. Paul and his disciples was more in evidence than Anselmian theory (which is reflected in a passing mention of satisfaction). To illustrate: all who are born of Adam contract unrighteousness (*iniustitia*) as their own in (or at) their conception (not, note, *by* their conception); thus,

> They would never have been justified except through rebirth in Christ, for this rebirth bestows on them through the merit of his passion the grace by which they are justified. For this benefit the Apostle exhorts us always to give thanks to the Father 'who has made us worthy [Vulg., *dignos*; Gk., *hikanosanti*, "fit," "capable"] to share the lot of the saints in light' [Colossians 1:12], and who has rescued us from the power of darkness and transferred us into the kingdom of his beloved Son, in whom we have redemption and remission of sins [Colossians 1:13f.][10].... Justification is a passing from the state in which a person is born an offspring of the first Adam, to the state of grace and 'of the adoption of sons' [Romans 8:15; *huiothesia*] of God, through the second Adam, Jesus Christ our Savior."[11]

Besides the terms *iustitia* (righteousness) and *renascentia* (rebirth) as descriptions of the new human condition, the Decree employs "new life," "redemption" and "the gift of the

---

[10]Ch. 3, *ibid.*, 795 [1523], p. 369; Clarkson, *ibid.*
[11]Ch. 4, *ibid.*, 796 [1524], p. 370; Clarkson, pp. 231-32.

Holy Spirit," all with appropriate New Testament citations. As to how the gift is received by adults, God's unmerited call is named as the beginning of justification. "Awakened and assisted by [God's] grace [they are] disposed to turn to their own justification by freely assenting to and cooperating with that grace. The result is that, when God touches the human heart with the illumination of the Holy Spirit, those who accept that inspiration certainly do something, since they could reject it; on the other hand, by their own free will, without God's grace, they could not take one step toward righteousness in God's sight."[12] Justification itself is said to follow upon the disposition or preparation spoken of,[13] but all begins with God's prevenient grace.[14] Nothing precedes it. No human act of disposition or preparation is contemplated without it. Justification is described as not only the remission of sins but sanctification and renewal of the interior individual through the voluntary reception of grace and gifts, whereby a person becomes righteous instead of unrighteous and a friend instead of an enemy, so as to become "an heir in the hope of life everlasting" [Titus 3:7].[15] Much more is said about how sinners are made righteous and continue in God's friendship. As to what made this possible, the Decree resorts to the Aristotelian four causes, supported by Pauline citations—although some council fathers unsuccessfully opposed this scholastic usage. After identifying the final and efficient causes but before the instrumental and formal causes, the Decree added as the meritorious cause the passion of Christ. Those who are justified share in these merits from the justice of God which renders us just.[16] In sum, it is the sufferings and death of Christ as believed in which the Tridentine teaching identifies as bringing about human salvation.

Certain propositions that were to have a lively history long

---

[12] *Ibid.*, 797 [1525], p. 370; Clarkson, p. 232 (adapted).

[13] *Ibid.*, 799 [1528], p. 371; Clarkson, p. 233.

[14] *Ibid.*, 797 [1525], p. 370; Clarkson, p. 232.

[15] See *ibid.*, 799 [1528], p. 37; Clarkson, p. 233.

[16] See *ibid.*, 799 [1529], p. 37; Clarkson, pp. 233-34.

after the Council of Trent were condemned as not being part of Catholic faith. Among these were believing with absolute certainty that one is absolved or justified; that no one is truly justified except the one who believes that s/he is; and that absolution and justification are effected by this faith alone. The canons deny, further, that anyone can be absolutely sure of persevering in grace or that, once justified, cannot lose grace. Quoted against any such presumption are 1 Corinthians 10:12, Philippians 2:12 and 2 Corinthians 6:3ff., "although all ought to have most secure hope in the help of God."[17]

Much more could be said about the Catholic response to the challenge of the Reformers as the fathers of Trent perceived it. The previous twenty-five years had been marked by argument and excommunication, pamphleteering and breaking with the Church on a previously unprecedented scale. Many theological opinions which had been acceptable as speculation had hardened into doctrines. These proved the infidelity of the "papalists" by their not espousing them. Charge and counter-charge concerned chiefly what Paul and the evangelists meant when they spoke, in the Vulgate translation, about "faith" (or "trust"), "conversion," "repentance" (or "penance") and "perseverance." Any observer or participant in the struggles of the times would have been right to say, "Things fall apart." But one center *did* hold. The fixèd star was the conviction of all parties that salvation was caused by the merits Christ won on Calvary and these alone. Any other New Testament reading of the redemptive mystery faded into the background. When, after confession, people made penitential satisfaction for sins it was rendered "to God through the merits of Christ."[18] Christian Europe had had its thoughts fixed on the death of Christ for the nine hundred years since Isidore of Seville (often called the last Church father of the West). It did not relinquish this lodestar no matter how much what was once thought certain was seen adrift.

---

[17]*Ibid.*, 806 [1541], p. 375; Clarkson, p. 238.

[18]*Ibid.* Session XIV, can. 13, 1713 [923], p. 403; Clarkson, p. 317; cf. Ch. 8, "Teaching on the Sacrament of Penance," 1691, 1692 [905] and "On Works of Satisfaction," 1693 [906]; cf. Clarkson, pp. 313-14.

Amazingly, Anselm's definition of the atonement as an act of satisfaction rendered by the death of Christ, although unscriptural, was universally assumed by the Reformers to be true. This was probably because of its basis in Chalcedon, which they took to be the correct expression of New Testament christology. It remained for unitarian—or antitrinitarian—thinkers like Michele Servet (d. 1553) and Fausto Sozzini (d. 1604) to attack the definition as baseless. The latter wrote a *Catechism* in which he devoted a chapter to the doctrine of satisfaction. He charged it with detracting from the mercy of God by teaching that Christ was the price for our sins and the one who placated the wrath of God when, in fact, God had forgiven by sheer mercy. Jesus had "taught" the way of salvation and "declared" the love of God, reconciling the world to God (as 2 Corinthians 5:19 says) by his death as a kind of martyr, but not God to the world. If Jesus did no more than reveal the divine mercy he did not have to be a divine person exercising it, as indeed Sozzini thought he was not. Similarly, the entire New Testament language on which the "common and orthodox" Anselmian doctrine (so the Swiss Reformed theologian Bullinger) was based—terms like "mediator"—was, he thought, entirely metaphorical.

As early as the Confession of Augsburg, which Philip Melanchthon drew up to make the Lutheran case at a Diet summoned by the emperor Charles V in 1530, Article IV "Of Justification" said that humans "are received into grace and their sins are remitted on account of Christ who makes satisfaction for sins on our behalf by his death."[19] The Jesuit theologian and cardinal Roberto Bellarmino (d. 1621) quoted an *Apology of the Confession of Augsburg* in support of agreement between Catholics and heretics, as he counted the Reformers, that the death of Christ was a satisfaction offered on the cross for the guilt of the whole human race.[20] The latter phrase was not an accurate description of all positions, how-

---

[19] Bettenson, *op. cit.*, p. 295.

[20] Cited by Pelikan, *4. Reformation of Church and Dogma (1300-1700)*, p. 359, where full citation of the Latin *Disputations on the Controversies* is supplied.

ever, since Reformed documents like the Helvetic Consensus
of 1675 reiterated the Calvinist position that "Christ in His
death was substituted as an expiatory sacrifice ... for none
but the elect [whom the Father] gave to Christ to be redeemed."[21] Still, the Catholic and Protestant consensus on the
satisfaction made to God for human sins by Christ on the
cross remained firm, despite the absence of the word "satisfaction" from Scripture. It was strengthened if anything by the
devotional works of Luther and the piety of Catholic reformers
like Philip Neri, Ignatius of Loyola and Teresa of Avila, all of
whom found a measure of satisfaction offered to the offended
justice of God in every deed of the human Christ. Luther is
credited with "rediscovering" the patristic view of the atonement, namely the defeat of sin, death and the devil by the
victorious Christ who is the righteousness of God, in what was
in effect a dislodging of the "rational" Latin doctrine of the
atonement.[22] But the debates of the Reformation period did
more to confirm the Anselmian theory of satisfaction than
loosen its hold.

The Dutch jurist Huig de Groot (Grotius, d. 1645) took on
Socinius of Siena by proposing a divinely authored plan of
atonement in which satisfaction was seen as a New Testament
reality but one that had no shadow of appeasement of the
divine wrath. Christ's death simply manifested the retributive
justice of God as regards sins.[23] Grotius is best known as a
disciple of his fellow Hollander Jacob Arminius (d. 1609) who
challenged Calvin's "fictitious fate of [double] predestination."
Arminianism is dismissed as a heresy no better than
Pelagianism in Calvinist writings but, with its insistence that as

---

[21] *The Helvetic Consensus Formula XIII* in John H. Leith, ed., *Creeds of the Churches* (New York: Doubleday Anchor Books, 1963), p. 315.

[22] See Gustav Aulén, *Christus Victor*, esp. Ch. 6, "Luther" (New York: Macmillan Paperbacks, 1969), pp. 101-22. Aulén euphorically describes Luther as having revived "the old classic theme of the Atonement as taught by the Fathers, but with a greater depth of treatment" (p. 102), but then disappoints by stressing only his love of conflict, drama, colors, and the devil as a personal surrogate for sin and death.

[23] Hugo Grotius, *Defense of the Catholic Faith concerning the Satisfaction of Christ* 1;4, cited by Pelikan 4:360-61.

part of human freedom there is no such thing as irresistible grace, it is largely the Catholic position. Arminius' view was spelled out in a *Remonstrant Confession* of 1610 to which the Synod of Dort (1618-19) responded vigorously. It did not make its way into Protestant thought widely until John Wesley (d. 1791) proposed it as the better reading of the church fathers, Augustine excepted. Jonathan Edwards of Northampton, Massachusetts (d. 1758) defended the traditional Reformed position in his essay *Original Sin* (posthumous), thereby setting the stage for some bitter argumentation among Protestants on the American frontier.

There has been nothing said up until now of one of the chief actors in the drama of the doctrine of salvation. It is the spirit of individualism, a distinct phenomenon from the centuries-old Christian concern for the individual. Augustine had an important part to play in it as a theological reality with his introspective *Confessiones* but even more his *Civitas Dei*, "the last great apology." This was in a sense the death-knell of the first three Christian centuries with their stress on the inbreaking of something new in human history—what has been called "the Constantinian turn." At the first preaching of the gospel there was the presence of Jesus, then the expectation of God's imminent reign, and finally a Church life of the presence of the Spirit that stood for it as symbolic. Augustine's city of God, however, has been present since the creation. Its genuine location is "above" and its true reality is future. Its citizens dwell here below in exile. As Gerhard Lohfink observes, the appearance of Christ hardly changes anything in this realm which stretches from the beginning to the end of human history.[24] Life begins with the resurrection of the dead: "Christ ... slowly withdraws his family from a world everywhere infected with ... evils and going to ruin, in order with that family to establish a city everlasting."[25] As this family withdraws it does not seem aware of its calling as a counter-

---

[24]Gerhard Lohfink, *Jesus and Community* (Philadelphia: Fortress, 1984), p. 184, bringing attention to *Civitas Dei* 12.28; 15.1; 17.1.

[25]Aurelius Augustinus, *City of God* 2.18, tr. by G.E. McCracken, Loeb Classical Library (Cambridge: Harvard University Press), I, 207.

cultural sign to the nations, only of its "rejoicing in hope insofar as that joy is wholesome."[26] As to the neoplatonic author of this and numerous masterpieces of the Christian West, he summed up all his desires in an early dialogue with Reason:

> "*A*. I desire to know God and the soul."
> "*R*. Nothing more?"
> "*A*. Absolutely nothing."[27]

The possibility of thinking individually rather than in community was a coefficient of the economic development of society. The flourishing of the individualist spirit is generally traced to the middle ages with the rise of the cities, an emerging artisan class, and the resultant awareness of oneself and one's capabilities as distinct from one's language group, clan and family. Emphasis on the individual grew during the renaissance of the twelfth century and experienced a resurgence in the fifteenth with increased literacy and, toward the end of that century, printing in movable type. The language in which the theological debates of the last chapter and this were carried on shows the overriding concern for the individual soul's salvation—arising safely with the saints above, in Augustine's phrase, to receive the promised kingdom. A sense of being a community of "the saints" whose redeemed condition as the body of Christ is a daily reality diminished correspondingly. Christians had always lived in hope of their personal deliverance from sin and its consequences. In the West they came to think of "being saved" as exclusively a matter of getting to heaven and escaping the punishments of hell. The Eastern churches lived in more disadvantaged human situations, often with Islam surrounding them or at their backs, but the texts of their liturgies in the vernacular sustained their votaries in a way that Latin worship did not do. The divine liturgy kept alive the corporate biblical and patristic idea of a people redeemed, more than individuals in lonely exile awaiting translation to another sphere.

[26] *Ibid.*, 18.49, tr. W.C. Green, VI, 61.

[27] *Soliloquies* 2.7, tr. T.F. Gilligan (New York: CIMA, "Fathers of the Church," 1948), I.2, p. 350.

The radical re-baptizers who preceded the Lutheran reform, priests like the Swiss Balthasar Hübmaier (d. 1528) and the Dutch Menno Simons (d. 1561), held that a close following of Christ or discipleship was the chief requisite for salvation, which they defined as a participation in the nature of God. A century later (Philipp) Jakob Spener (d. 1705), a Lutheran pietist theologian, would write a treatise called *Heartfelt Desire* (1675) in which he identified as the foundation stone of salvation a close kinship between Jesus Christ and all humanity, to whom Christ was brother. He depended much on the mystical classic of Johannes Arndt, *True Christianity* (1605-09), in reaction to the Lutheran scholastic "orthodoxy" that put its stamp on the seventeenth century. Spener influenced King Frederick of Prussia to found the University of Halle, where August Hermann Francke and his son were successively professors. Johann Albrecht Bengel was the leader of another school of pietism in Württemberg. These earnest men of experience or, as we would call it existential concern, increasingly put the questions, "When was I first aware of my rebirth in Christ?" and, "How do I know I am saved?" Their answer came, needless to say, in subjective terms but also, perhaps surprisingly, in charitable good works as the fruit of their piety.

These groups were zealous in spreading the gospel, with the added component of a rigid code of "Christian behavior." This included the now familiar prohibitions of dancing, card playing and other forms of recreation or stimulation of the senses as well as the fullness of gospel morality. The Lutheran pietist "little churches" which gave birth to numerous sects like the Moravians and various groups of Brethren were marked by a spirit of separation from the world, although not by the conviction that all but they were damned. The same was not true of the Puritan strain in the Church of England. There, the influential Reformed theology strove to eliminate all remaining Catholic elements. Article XVII of the Thirty-nine Articles had carefully avoided expressing belief in double predestination but the Westminster [Abbey] Confession of 1646 affirmed it, saying that those "not elected ... cannot be saved; much less can men, not professing the Christian religion, be saved in any other way whatsoever, be they never so diligent to frame their lives according to the light of nature and the law of that religion they do profess; and to assert and maintain that they may is very pernicious, and to be detested." The separatist spirit of the Lutheran pietists and continental anabaptists marked the English Puritans and free church dissidents (later "Baptists") who came earlier to the North American colonies than the German Lutherans and anabaptists. It was not evident culturally, however, because, unlike the Mennonites, Amish, and Brethren, those of English stock *were* the establishment.

The Language of Salvation Since the Reformation

After the extensive historical development of the last few chapters a summing up of the Western views of salvation that came to prevail is indicated.

(A). *Catholic* theology and piety seems a place to begin. There was, first of all, the conviction that Jesus had been given as a gift by God to die for the sins of the world, a death he had undergone willingly. The effects of this redemptive death were universal; it was not thought to have been done only for those whom God elected for salvation, although not all in the event might be saved. In the Latin liturgy which was preached to the people despite their ignorance of the language, Jesus Christ was praised twice for having taken away "the sins of the world," once in the *Gloria* or greater doxology and again as the body and blood of Christ were held aloft in the communion rite. The word "sins" was in the plural (*peccata*), different from the singular of John 1:29 in which the Baptist said the Lamb of God had come to take away a world's sin (*hamartian*) and different from the same word and concept in the singular used throughout Paul's letters. For Paul, "sins" in the plural is always *paraptōmata*, usually rendered literally as "transgressions." This meant that the Lucan description in Acts of Jesus' death "for the forgiveness of sins" had won out in the popular mind, which the liturgy both reflects and conveys. The sins spoken of were surely meant to include original sin, i.e., the sin each child was accounted guilty of at origin or birth, and all sins committed thereafter as a consequence of that inheritance. If one asked, or asks, a Catholic, "What sins does Jesus take away?" the answer the questioner receives will probably be "our sins" with an emphasis on actual offenses.

Pressing the believer in that exchange, one might go on to ask, "How *does* Jesus' death achieve the taking away of our sins?" to which one would receive a variety of answers. But they would fall within this range: "God accepted the sufferings and death of Jesus on the cross to save us" [no further explanation given]. Or the same but with the added phrase, "to take away original sin"; "to open the gates of paradise which had been closed since Adam's sin" [pure Augustine, found in most catechisms of the last four hundred years]; "to save us from our sins." The substitution theory which flourished in the later middle ages did not, by and large, survive Trent. Few Catholics would be likely to answser, "Christ died in our place," or, "He accepted on Calvary the punishments we deserve" (even though the phrase "sinless in the sinner's stead" occurs in the popular paschal hymnody of all the languages). There would be reflected, rather, a modified version of Anselm's theory in the following sense. Catholics would know that Christ's sufferings as a human being were what made Calvary effective before God, but also that if he were not the Son of God (they would say "God," not distinguishing among the persons) it would not have worked quite as it did. The thing that has dropped out of Catholic consciousness in the Anselmian formula is the notion of necessity. There would simply be silence about it. If the inquirer were to press further on this point an Ockhamist/Scotist answer would be forthcoming: "God worked it out that way" or "The sacrifice Jesus freely offered on the cross was part of God's plan for our redemption"; in brief, "most fittingly" would unconsciously win out over "necessarily." Also, in Catholic speech the blood of Christ shed upon the cross or Christ's most precious blood would appear as a description of the redemptive deed rather than the one-word symbols "Calvary" or "the Cross." But this is a matter of religious rhetoric.

To continue, Catholics would not until very recently couple the resurrection with the crucifixion as having achieved atonement or a reconciliation with God. For over a thousand years

Western Christians have distinguished between the two mysteries, making the resurrection—as an apologetic matter—a proof of Christ's divinity, or seeing it as a divine manifestation that something has already been achieved. The one paschal mystery of the biblical and patristic ages has not been viewed as one in the West for a long time.

Any discussion of salvation among Catholics from the simplest grade school children to papal theologians would identify its center of gravity in the life to come. At present, graced status would by all means be acknowledged but in an exchange on salvation it would be spoken of in the relation of seed to flower or acorn to oak. The notion of present deification, even Pauline life "in Christ" or "in the Spirit," would not be proffered immediately if at all.

The pneumatology of Western Christians is notoriously weak. It is coming to the fore in Catholic charismatic circles in the last decades but in a strange and not always traditional way. The Holy Spirit proves to be, in conversation even with leaders of the movement, not the fullness of deity poured out on the whole Church which believes in the resurrection, but a divine person distinct from the other two who dwells in individuals constantly given to speaking of this Spirit—sometimes as if not all the baptized were similarly endowed. Spirit-knowledge had a gnostic tinge in Montanist, Anabaptist and pietist Protestant circles (add in Joachim of Fiore and the spiritual Franciscans) which is not entirely absent in its current Catholic manifestation. In the Christian East the Spirit's presence has always been a mystery of the Church rather than the possession of knowing individuals; so too in the liturgy and—weakly—in the theology of the Catholic West, if not its popular piety.

Does the unique priesthood of Christ figure in the Catholic outlook on the redemptive mystery? Yes, but not strongly. This is not because a human priesthood or the cult of Mary and the saints detracts from the office of the one high priest, as opponents of the Catholic Church are convinced, but because insistence on his victimhood is so much to the fore. Jesus Christ is for Catholics supremely the one offered and only secondarily the offerer. The stress of the Reformers on the redemptive theology of the epistle to the Hebrews was influential here. They employed it as part of polemic against an ordained priesthood. Understandably, the Catholic response was not to feature the writing lest its stress on Christ as the mediator of a new covenant (see Hebrews 8:6; 9:15; 12:24) or "one mediator" (1 Timothy 2:5) be taken as a threat to a human priesthood. In fact, the priesthood of all believers traceable to 1 Peter 2:5, 9 would logically seem to be much more threatened by the texts of the "one mediator" since the baptized are much more numerous than the ordained. But in religious arguments logic does not always prevail. One's point of departure does.

The 1948 encyclical letter of Pope Pius XII on the sacred liturgy was entitled *Mediator Dei*, its opening words. It spoke freely of Christ as the one intermediary who achieved human salvation. The epistle to the Hebrews likewise has a prominent part in the three-year cycle of lectionary readings, which should ensure some exposition of its theology wherever Catholic preaching is taken seriously.

Two other negative factors need mentioning, one regrettable, the other far less so. First, one does not find in Catholic theology generally the peculiar contribution of St. Paul to the exposition of salvation in Christ. This is *not* the biblical image of a ransom price or the sacrifice of Christ's life rather than that of beasts in the temple. These images were firmly fixed in the tradition when Paul came to believe. He adopted and promoted them. And, although the figure of justification is peculiar to Paul, it is not his greatest contribution. This is true if only because it has been presented as if, being only a part, it were the whole. As Schweitzer pointed out, the Church is chiefly indebted to Paul for his theology of two ages or eons, one of darkness in Adam, another of light in Christ. To be a people of the new and final epoch is the glory of Christians so long as they confidently put no one who has lived since Christ, the Jews least of all, firmly in the former age. The Pauline letters to the Colossians and Ephesians are authentically in his spirit, as the meaning of outreach to a pagan world came home to the authors. They view the whole world as renewed in Christ. The full implications of the apostle's Adam-Christ typology were first discerned by Irenaeus who was both read and misread by Origen, the last fullscale patristic apocalyptist. A totally new life in a new age captures best the teaching of Jesus which John and Paul comprehended and passed along. The gospel when authentically preached sees the present of the Spirit in the light of the future—God's future in which Jesus will be revealed to the world as the Christ. This New Testament view of salvation as a transfer of kingdoms or lordships has always had an existence in the Church Catholic and Orthodox, if at times a muted and even fugitive one. If self-renewal in light of the past is a constant, the future of this doctrine is bright.

The second non-feature of Catholic teaching on salvation is Christ's victory over the devil. Over sin, yes, and over death which is a reminder of sin's power in us. But Satan and the demons of hell, while believed in, have not had the prominence in Catholic soteriology since Trent that they did in the time of the fathers or the late middle ages (i.e., the Reformation).

Finally, when Catholic express their faith in redemption in Christ, they speak freely of their cooperation in it, or what God expects of them as part of it. They are conscious of a heavy responsibility to stay faithful to the commandments of God and of Christ if at the judgment they are to be "with the Lord." They do not shrink from the language of "merit" or being found "worthy" since they know that all their merits are Christ's. It is he who lives in them to enable their freedom to the fullest. They think of prayer including sacramental prayer, fasting, almsgiving and the spiritual and corporal works of mercy as incumbent on them if they are to live out their salvation. None of these is thought of as a human "work" proceeding from sin, to be set at odds with faith, but as "faith working through love." Galatians 5:6 is a text which Trent cited more than once. As to earthly and heavenly intercessors who can be called on to assist in achieving salvation, they are not abjured on a scriptural principle but called on freely—all of them living images of Christ and the Spirit, none of them a threat to Christ's mediation or to God as the "author and finisher of our faith" (Hebrews 12:2).

The social aspect of salvation in the Catholic view was

chiefly life in the Church, the body of Christ, set against life in "the world," those outside. Even in the days between the fourth and seventh centuries when there began to be something like a Catholic Europe, with Jews an unassimilated body in the midst and Muslims at the edges, this culture developed into one divided along the lines of the figure of the two swords in Gethsemane (see Luke 22:38), designated the sword of the spirit and the secular arm. Because popes and bishops were so wary of kings and princes, and vice versa, a delicate balance was achieved in which the rights of the Church and of the body politic were jealously guarded.Political philosophers like Aquinas and Dante wrote on the common good and the rule of princes.A care for all on the earth or even the earth itself was beyond their power to imagine. They would have admitted without hesitation that the effects of the redemption were cosmic, but what this meant as a demand on the Church as Church in practice, Catholics of the medieval and Renaissance worlds would not have been able to say. Only in the last century did the Western Church come to widespread social consciousness—spurred no little by the anti-religious socialist threat—that human salvation was very much a matter of the here and now. The conditions of human dignity had to be met, without which no one could hear or heed the gospel.

(B). An attempt to summarize *Protestant* convictions about a redeemed humanity cannot be done in global fashion so well as in evangelical (Lutheran), reformed (Calvinist) and radical (Anabaptist) categories. Since many of these distinctions have already been made we shall spell out what in the tradition is common to all three and distinguish it from another that began to flourish in the last century: a conservative evangelicalism that lies outside the churches or, if within them, is scarcely incorporated into their faith and life. The Protestant view of salvation is that the terms of this pure and unmerited gift of God are so clearly laid out in Scripture that only a person resisting the promptings of the Holy Spirit can fail to see it there. No one ordained to any ministry but that of teaching the Bible is of any use in guiding to salvation, nor are sacraments the channels of the grace of salvation. Only faith is of any avail, faith in what God has done for a world, not merely of sinners but of the ungodly (see Romans 5:6).

Out of love for sinners and unbounded mercy, God sent his only Son to die on the cross, receiving the punishments that our sins deserve. We have been alienated from God since the day of Adam's fall and come to birth as children of wrath, incapable of doing anything on our own that does not have the character of sin. All our works are evil and would forever be, had God not chosen to overlook our transgressions and accept instead the unique merits of the Son on our behalf. This Jesus by his obedient death on the cross caused God to see in us what God sees in him, namely the author of an all-sufficient sacrifice which reconciles us to God by God's accepting it as ours. The acceptance in faith of what Christ has done for us is an exercise of absolute trust to which God impels us by prevenient grace. It gives the blessed assurance that we are justified in God's sight and cannot decline from that initial state of righteousness. If we should sin grievously thereafter this establishes that our faith was insufficient, for genuine justifying faith gives assurance of salvation and cannot be departed from.

It includes total repentance of sins. No further penitential acts are necessary. They would not only be fruitless but an impugning of the initial gift of justification. The life of justified sinners (who remain sinners while at the same time just) is marked by the lifetime expression of sorrow for sin and the performance of good works. These are the fruits of a justified life and in no sense contributory to righteousness, a matter which only faith in the all-sufficient merits of Christ can achieve. A holy life is incumbent on the justified sinner but this holiness is Christ's, not the individual's.

In brief it is best to say that anything the New Testament says about the mystery of redemption is Protestant faith in it and nothing that any subsequent age said or did about it is that faith. Since, however, so much is said in Scripture— Chapter 2 reports only a portion of that tapestry—we can identify three organizing themes that underlie Protestant conviction about the mystery: (a). The christology of the Bible is basically a soteriology (Chalcedonian-Anselmian in fact, but thought to be self-evident to people of faith in God's word), which assures the salvation of those who have faith in the merits Christ won on the cross; the righteous elect of God cannot fall away from their elect status but must continue to do the works of God as signs of that election; the sure sign that one is on the way to salvation, not destruction, is the close following of Christ in his teaching and example which accompanies justifying faith in the cross. (b). Salvation is as much a matter of the life to come in the Protestant tradition as the Catholic, but there is the consciousness in this life that one is justified although a sinner, or among the elect and hence "saved." (c). There has been little more awareness in Protestant theology than in Catholic that belief in redemption brings with it a strong responsibility to achieve in society the conditions of the life of the redeemed (the Wesleyan tradition is an exception). Anticipating the rule of God to come by a corporate life which attempts to reduce want, hunger, wars and disease is not a hallmark of Protestant piety, although the commitment of the anabaptist churches to peace stands out as an exception. Missionary activity is accompanied by much striving to relieve human need but usually out of compassion rather than on a redemptive principle. Getting non-Christians to know the Bible and profess faith in its saving message is the primary way to spread the benefits of the redemption, as the Protestant churches conceive it.

(C). The *conservative evangelical* or *fundamentalist* tradition might be described as Reformed faith in all its purity except that it has no need to recall any previous chapter of Christian history. Its reliance on the saving word of an inerrant Bible is total. Nothing that people who call themselves "Christians" do is authentically such if they do not believe in the inerrancy of Scripture. This means that the believers who can claim the name Christian are those who have that faith. None but Christians thus defined can expect to be saved. Others can expect to be lost eternally, suffering the pains of hell at the hands of a just God whether they have heard the gospel or not, because their sins, original and actual, deserve such retribution. Reliance on a priesthood or sacraments or acts of repentance are a relapse into Judaistic or pagan practice, betraying an insufficient trust in the merits of Christ. Everything that the New Testament says about preaching and faith and prayer must be done; nothing that it does not say may be done. The Acts of the Apostles and the activity described in the Pauline letters (all fourteen, Hebrews included) are historical in every detail and must be replicated by Christian assemblies. Failure to do so will ensure the "second death" and the "lake of fire" of Revelation 20:6, 15. The fundamentalist spirit is interested in the salvation of individuals who, once saved, assemble as a gathering of the saved. They can clearly remember the day this blessed condition overtook them, since they experienced so unmistakably God's call and the exact time of their response in choosing Christ as their personal savior. The mutual support of community members by works of love is part of the faith of biblical inerrantists but they resist any supposition that corporate social action is required to manifest the world's redeemed condition. They are even likely to view it as a godless substitution of works for faith and as impugning faith in the life to come when all will be changed. These believers are rigidly apocalyptic, taking all the imagery of the utterances of Jesus, Paul, and the book of Revelation literally. Those who labor for the improvement of life on earth as a gospel imperative may very well not believe in "a new heavens and a new earth." In any case, they are wasting valuable time that could be given to spreading the biblical word as they improve the shape of this world, which is only passing away.

Before the summary of three general Protestant ways of looking at salvation is concluded, the paradox should be observed that those who are theologically suspicious of good works often excel in them, while those who praise them unhesitatingly often institutionalize them rather than build them into the fabric of everyday congregational life. There are, of course, notable exceptions to this generalization on both the Catholic and Protestant sides. Two things happened in the last century to change the outlook of both major communions—though not the smaller sects in America—on the ethical demands imposed by belief in human salvation as something already achieved from God's side. The first was the socialist challenge of Marx and Engels, atheistic in implication if not by theoretical necessity, that religion was a set of empty promises about the future which lulled the masses and gave free play to the propertied classes to exploit the poor. The riots of the proletariat against the amassers of capital in mid-century were inevitably violent but it was not this violence that caused Catholic social theorists and later, popes, to react theologically to the Marxist threat. It was the claim that nothing in the gospel had any real consequences for the lives of the oppressed and landless poor, that religion could only offer the empty consolation that a blissful eternity lay ahead.

The Catholic response was much more theoretical than actual because of the resistance of Catholic capital to papal teaching. Loud protests in favor of the rights of ownership against a Church that had "gone socialist" were raised in the last century and this. In fact, the social theory proposed in favor of decent wages as the fruits of labor and an equitable distribution of the goods of the earth was based on the eternal law of God, *ius naturale*, rather than humanity's status as redeemed. The Protestants of Europe were under siege on other fronts and did not align themselves with this protest, as indeed they perhaps could not in light of their repudiation of any natural law ethic as compatible with the gospel. It remained for Catholics of the present century in Latin America, often persons with European theological educations, to construct the beginnings of a theology of liberation in which liberation means redemption here on earth if faith in it hereafter is to be credible to the masses.

The outcry against the betrayal of the gospel by the importation of Marxism in religious guise has been long and loud. The reason is twofold: salvation has such a vigorous history as a matter of the life to come that any claim for its necessary implications for this life can be seen as denying faith in eternal life; and the theorists of liberation theology have so stressed a gospel ethic that a systematic theology of the implications of the redemption for this life has either gone undone or been substituted for by an at times oversimplified exegesis of the Bible.

The second movement was the so-called liberal theology of the nineteenth-century Protestant European universities which deemphasized the doctrinal differences among the traditions and even the basic soteriological theory on which the Reformation was built. The liberty of interpretation of Scripture was by no means denied, but the critical study of the Bible managed to dethrone systematics, bringing with it a concern to live according to gospel morality interpreted in Kantian (later existential) categories rather than to emphasize fine points of doctrine. The liberal spirit had a general loosening effect on the commitment of the churches to their traditional positions. Ritschl and Harnack were representative voices of this movement with Bultmann and his school following shortly after the 1914-18 War. In the United States, the "social gospel" associated with Walter Rauschenbusch and afterward the Niebuhrs similarly raised Protestant consciousness about ethics and society. The appeal, as in Europe, was to the imperative of the gospel to live morally, which meant socially as well as individually. But the doctrine of human redemption was not enlisted as the primary motivating force.

In the last few decades some U.S. Protestant evangelicals of low ecclesiology but high commitment to traditional soteriology have departed sharply from the individualism and total abstention from social action that marks most of their number. They have taken on many issues besides the opposition to war and violence that characterizes their anabaptist origins, chiefly world hunger and health in the third and fourth worlds. Without attending to who may or may not be "saved," they seek to raise consciousness about human need everywhere. Like the liberation theology movement with which they are allied in spirit, these evangelicals look to the mystery of human redemption as the basis for their efforts.

A Usable Theology of Salvation for Our Day

Christian symbols of salvation, verbal and non-verbal, are so rich and varied—starting with the Bible and coming through the centuries—that one could be discouraged at the prospect of choosing among them the most serviceable for human use worldwide in the age that is upon us. How, in other words, can a theology of salvation be proposed that millions will live by? There are, of course, certain "givens." For all Christians, the God they worship is one who chose to be self-disclosed in Jesus, the Jew of Nazareth, whom they adore as Word of God, sole-begotten within the awesome reaches of deity. This Jesus to whom divine honors are accorded as Lord and Christ is the same who reveals in his humanity the compassion of God. Jesus Christ is the unique sacrament of God. At the same time he is the righteousness of God to the human race, the one who elevates it to a height greater than it had known at the creation. This he does through the power of the Holy Spirit whom he sent from the Father upon his return as the Risen One to the glory from which he came. Christians believe in a world that is suffused with the Spirit, a world that dwells in God and God in it as long as it has existed. That is what they mean by the mystery of creation; the existence of all that is not God in intimate relation with and continuing dependence on the God by whom it came to be. A first coming into being of our expanding universe is unimaginable to the simple and inconceivable to the learned. But all can derive meaning from the biblical story of a God who brought all into existence with effortless ease, not a cosmic struggle in which personified earth and sea and sky were rent violently apart. The most important thing about the first creation story, after its repeated insistence that all is the work of God, is the reiterated chant, "And God saw that it was good."

Enter the second creation story, the more primitive and less polished one, in which God is given the proper name that Israel knows its Lord by, YHVH. It has many insights to share about human life and character but chiefly this, that the human creature is flawed from the beginning. Capable of being creation's steward from the first day onward, he opts for mistrust of God, a self-reliance that borders on arrogance. After that there come in quick succession the fratricide of Cain, the mindless violence of Lamech, the *hubris* of the men of Babel and the deluge, a chaos that reverted to something of the formless waste which preceded the Spirit's hovering over the waters. These pictographic tales bear the full weight of what Pascal called *la gloire* and *la misère* of human freedom.

They and all the history of Israel that follows depict one thing: the need for redemption a free humanity has from the first moment of its creation. They are not two mysteries of creaturehood, they are one.

There is a third aspect of creaturely being. It is that, having been formed in the image and likeness of God, this person who can know and choose like God must be open to being holy like God—numinous, apart, yet merciful and just to fellow creatures—for this is to be godlike. In brief, creation, redemption and sanctification are not three works of God on human behalf but one: God in relation to humanity as God *must* be God and as God *freely chooses* to be God. Unlike the medievals, we know we cannot solve the mystery of the divine necessity and the divine liberty, not even by locating both tidily within the recesses of godhead.

Does Christianity look upon a creation that needs redeeming and sanctifying as much as, and for as long as, it needs continuing dependence on God for its being? It does or it should. Otherwise it will be in terrible straits over its conception of God and what the biblical tales of human origins are telling it. For whatever the Bible may say about the disobedience of the first Human (*ha Adam*) and his spouse Life (*Ḥayya*), the mother of all the living, it does not tell of a race created flawed so much as limited and free. What God does is well done, not imperfectly done. It is only humans, and angels, who have the tragic capacity to do badly what they are able to do well. A theologian we have called upon earlier speaks perceptively of what Christians believe when they say the world is in need of, and has been offered, redemption:

> The doctrine of creation is really the statement of a promise ... which is ingrained in the very nature and structure of the world.... The world's createdness ... is a pointer. It points to the possibility of the human world's becoming, in an open, explicit, and realized way, what it already is implicitly and in principle: God's world.... People talk about redemption, and about the need for redemption, because circumstances in the human world do not correspond with the promise of creation.... People are "tied and bound" in

relations and attitudes which make them hostile to God and to one another. To actualize the promise of creation therefore means necessarily, to put right something which is wrong.... To speak of redemption ... is to speak of the way God acts to fulfill the promise of creation. God does this by becoming present for people as his own Word, and so setting them free for life of a new quality—for a life fulfilled in love.[28]

The tying and binding to attitudes of hostility that Norris speaks of are human doing, not God's doing. God does not make a human creature who must hate but one who can choose to hate. Humanity's downfall is located in its freedom. But its fall from grace—the divine favor that invites it to be godlike—is not a necessary exercise. It is a tragically free one. The biblical story of human origins is the work of an Israelite people which had experienced God's favor toward it at every point in its corporate existence and its life as individuals. The Genesis authors—Spirit-led in all they wrote, as later generations were to see them—could not conceive of a time before Abraham and Sarah when humanity had not been the subject of God's tender concern. They composed a tale of primordial sin to describe the mystery long reflected on of a creation that was redeemed from the outset. "God acts to fulfill the promise of creation" from the first moment there is need. There is need from the time any angel or human could have done what was most in creaturely interest and did not do it. The biblical author identifies that time as the first human moment, even as an apocryphal author would later see it in the angelic, when it was said to God: "I will not serve." Creation and redemption are one in Genesis 1—3, just as is the sanctification of the human pair. There is a counterthrust on the creature's part but the action of God on human behalf goes uninterrupted.

From the time that non-Semitic Christians began to take their holy books as history—and they did so to oppose the myths of the Greeks as insubstantial deceits—they got into

<hr />

[28]Norris, *op. cit.*, pp. 71, 73.

difficulties which the biblical writers would have been incapable
of. They devised the problem of Adam's state before he sinned
as contrasted with after. This led to speculation about a state
of primordial grace of which the pair was stripped. Some
thought it a being reduced to a condition of "pure nature."
Initial elevation to a graced state was followed by a "fall." This
resort to spatial metaphor led to the pre- and post-lapsarian
disputes (temporal metaphor, though thought to be historical)
which betrayed an unwarranted confidence in a knowledge of
how things were, both at the start and immediately after
Adam's sin. To be sure, the ejection from Eden and threefold
sentence of God delivered to the snake, the woman and the
man (Genesis 3:24, 14-19) tells of a sharply worsened condition
of all creation. But to take the story as a detailed description of
early days and weeks is surely wrong, still more to see in it an
account of God's withholding grace or favor from the whole
human race until Christ should come. That was to read the
sacred page in a way that St. Paul did not. He only wished to
contrast a disadvantaged life without faith in Christ with a life
of faith in him. To describe humanity, and above all the Jews,
as lacking in redemptive grace over the ages would have struck
him as an outrage. We can almost see Paul railing at the more
literal minded interpreters of Augustine, at this perversion of
Augustine's fleshing out of the Adam myth with an Adam-
Christ myth.

Redemption for the Christian is, to be sure, promise in
Adam and fulfillment in Christ. That is to say, however, that
human unfulfillment—sin—which is as old as human life—is
the tragic choice of human freedom from which God as its
author can never be divorced, having made a creature capable
of it. There has been the need of a redeemed world and a saved
human race for as long as there has been such a world and
race. God, being God, has never for an instant been absent,
failing to supply that need, since who more than God would
wish to see the promise of creation fulfilled? There lay ahead
for human ages a fullness of redemption in Christ. But there
was always redemption. And it was there for all, not only for
those to whom God was self-revealed, as to the Hebrews. The
Jews who wrote the Bible and the Christians who added their

Scriptures to this collection surely shortened God's arm by confining the divine graciousness to the self-disclosures that had been shared with them. God has never been bound by such necessity. The better truth, as a few Jews and a few Christians have always discerned, is that the redemptive grace of God is a reality of always and everywhere. There has not for an instant been an unredeemed world nor a person not called to fulfill the promise of creation, with or without a knowledge of Christ. Revelation grows. An awareness of its having been made to Israel and to the gentiles in Christ spreads. But God's redemptive love does not grow or change. That is a constant.

Salvation may therefore be described as the self-disclosure of God's will for the creation, which from the human side is a growing knowledge of the love God bears it. God's love for creatures is not, cannot be, a matter of more and less. It can only be a matter of human awareness of it. God is never inactive in human life—all human life and each human life. The call of Abraham was a deed of God of great magnitude. So was the Torah given to Moses. So too was the life, teaching and obedient death of Jesus in the spirit of this Instruction. Christians see in the person, life and death of Jesus the peak of self-disclosure of God's love for the human race, a love which they term redemptive or saving.

When believers in Jesus as the world's Savior say they know it is redeemed by the blood of his cross, and they redeemed as part of that world, they declare their inability to conceive of any revelation of God's love to match this one. It is not that God can say, "I love you as I never loved before." That is unthinkable. It is that in the person of Jesus Christ a human being responded to God's love as it had never been responded to before. By his obedience—a matter of freedom and not craven conformity—he fulfilled in himself the promise of creation. He did more. By the quality of his life and death he renewed the potential all human beings have for serving God and each other. They had lost the way to God and their own identity. He helped them find it in his own person with the simple Johannine declaration, "I am the way."

The Christian ages have found in Jesus' blood on Calvary the supreme symbol of his human love, which at the same time discloses the measure of the divine love. The blood, the painful death, has always been a symbol. Sometimes it is taken for the reality. This has led to certain confusions, the worst of which is the rejection of any talk of the love of God which can take such brutal form. But, as St. Anselm pointed out long ago, Jesus' death in its circumstances was but the factual outcome of a life lived the way he lived it—a life of total obedience. Put another way, it was a perfect human life, and God responded to it. Not its painful ending redeemed us but its totality: a life lived as people should live human life. Many Christians continue to take comfort in the symbol of the cross as perfectly expressive of the love God bears the human race. But others are less moved by it. They say that the symbol is violent and they cannot identify the God of peace with violence. They have been so drenched in cruel behavior and human slaughter that they wonder how one innocent death could have been of supreme importance.

Calvary connotes to some a deed of God done *for* people which they seem to have only to verbalize repeatedly in an exercise they call "faith," whereupon some marvelous transformation in them takes place. On another front, the cross continues to be understood erroneously by some Christians, and almost universally by Jews, as a reproach to the Jewish people because of the evangelists' location of guilt for Jesus' death in the Passover crowds and temple priesthood, not the Roman state. Partly because of this confusion, but for other better reasons, the mystery of redemption in Christ is increasingly symbolized in church art by representations of him risen from the tomb, arms outstretched in embrace as on the cross. The theology of St. Luke found in his gospel and Acts provides the lead here, with its presentation of the risen Christ as the cause of the remission of human sins if it is accepted in faith. For Luke the crucifixion is the necessary condition for the resurrection. This is a reading of the Christ-event in which those committed to medieval passion piety find an affront. But it is an aspect of authentic New Testament theology and it may have much to say to our time. An even stronger symbol for many is the teaching of Jesus, his message brought from God, which early compilers of "sayings-collections" before the canonical gospels proposed as the totality of his redeeming work, untranslated into the deed of the cross.

Most important of all, perhaps, is the dawning consciousness after many centuries that the redemption of creation means the achieving of God's plan for it in this world as a prelude to its final fulfillment. This takes salvation out of the category of a "religious" mystery available to the pious and places it squarely where it belongs as a *human* mystery. For God to save or to redeem is a rescue from death and hell only in terms of finality. Far short of that, it is a salvaging of humanity from realizing its worst possibilities in this life. These include the carnage men inflict on fellow men in wars and acts of economic violence, the plundering and pollution of the earth, and the expression of greed in all its forms, of which the perverted use of sex is but a part. To be "saved by the blood of the cross" is to be a human being. Consciously to be redeemed is to know something of the awe-full love God bears to every human creature. Accepting the implications of that love means doing something throughout life to make of life something that it might be for all: a place of human happiness that does not make a cruel joke of the concept of a blessed eternity. Salvation is a social reality or it is no reality at all. It is the beginning of God's dream for human society. Whoever claims that salvation touches the fate of individual believers only has not begun to grasp it.

Does this vision of the universality of redemption negate the uniqueness of Christ's sacrificial death, the special revelation that Christians are convinced has been given them, or the obligation to go into the whole world and bring the gospel to every creature? It does none of these things. What it does is destroy all false security deriving from presumed superiority as part of a greater ignorance of the mystery believed in. For the message of salvation in Christ can only be brought to people whom God has already been at work to save and well knows how to save, even if they never hear of Christ and the gospel. The burden of evangelizing is heavier, not lighter, on those who know that the gospel is a secular humanism in the sense that its first effect is to make human beings more human in this *saeculum* (this time, this place), which is their world. "First live," says the old Roman proverb, "then philosophize." Live humanly, says the true herald of the gospel. You might then know what to make of the life Jesus came to bring. Those two lives could even be one and the same.

One final matter remains which is of supreme importance. It is that salvation is wholly a matter of God's doing and wholly a matter of human doing. If this is not true the incarnation has no meaning. In Christian faith the world's Savior was the eternal Word of God who at the same time was fully human, one undivided person. The redeemed believer is not united to godhead with the same intimacy as Jesus, but unless there is a similar—not same—conjunction, no redemption can take place. If Jesus had not been obedient to God in the way he was there would have been no redemption of the kind there was. Similarly, there can be no human reception of the benefits of redemption without the full engagement of our wills. There is a heresy that denies this. In the Catholic West it was called "quietism" but it has an equally lively history in Orthodox and Protestant Christianity. One even hears it in Catholic circles of piety nowadays when, in the spirit of the age, one might expect at least one new and untried heresy. "In myself I accomplish nothing. It is God who achieves everything in me."

Nonsense! As pious disclaimer it may have some rhetorical significance but as theological statement it is bunk. Redeemed believers who have not responded with every faculty to the love held out to them have not been treated humanly by the God they mean to praise. They have been dealt with as automatons. A human race redeemed on those terms was scarcely worth the effort of creating. God wants a human response from human beings, just as God could only have looked on the Word eternally uttered as a beloved Son if that Jew Jesus had done everything the Father had commanded him. We are created apart from ourselves but we cannot be redeemed apart from ourselves. That would be inhuman. God cannot look on approvingly at anything inhuman in us, however much glory we may wish to render to God by our confusion.

Our treatment of the mystery of salvation needs to stop here. It is a mystery, hence impenetrable to the human mind, yet capable of some rational exploration. It is a supremely important mystery, perhaps *the* Christian mystery. For, whereas minor follies have been uttered in the name of salvation in the Christian past, they are as nothing compared to those of the current age. Whole populations are once more being complacently consigned to hell; marriages and families are being shipwrecked in the name of the gospel; and God is being regularly reduced from the boundless love that is godhead to a tiny despot interested only in his friends. Christian faith is both too large and too largeminded to be replaced by this puny caricature. Yet such perversion of the glorious reality "salvation" is happening globally among earnest cadres which preempt for themselves the rich self-denomination "Christian." This small book has been an attempt to describe the height and breadth and depth of the love of God expressed in Christ Jesus and in the Spirit which declares that humanity is no less than made like to God if it will respond humanly to this love.

Such is the unfathomable mystery of redemption.

Suggested Readings

Berryman, Philip, *Liberation Theology*. New York, 1987.

Burns, J. Patout, "The Economy of Salvation: Two Patristic Traditions," *Theological Studies* 37 (1976): 598-619.

_____, tr. and ed. *Theological Anthropology* (Irenaeus through Orange). Philadelphia, 1981.

Durrwell, F.X., *The Resurrection: A Biblical Study*. New York, 1960.

_____, *In the Redeeming Christ*. New York, 1963.

Fairweather, E.R., *A Scholastic Miscellany: Anselm to Occam*. Philadelphia, 1956.

Franks, Robert, *A History of the Doctrine of the Work of Christ in Its Ecclesiastical Development*. 2 vols., New York, 1918.

Grillmeier, Aloys, *Christ in Christian Tradition: From the Apostolic Age to Chalcedon (451)*. New York, 1965.

Lochman, Jan Milič, *Reconciliation and Liberation: Challenging a One Dimensional View of Salvation*. Philadelphia, 1980.

Lyonnet, Stanislas and Léopold Sabourin, *Sin, Redemption and Sacrifice: A Biblical and Patristic Study*. Rome, 1970.

McIntyre, John, *St. Anselm and His Critics. A Re-Interpretation of "Cur Deus Homo."* Edinburgh, 1954.

Metz, J.B., *The Emergent Church. The Future of Christianity in a Post-Bourgeois World*. New York, 1981.

Meyendorff, John, *Christ in Eastern Christian Thought*. New York, 1969.

Norris, Richard A., Jr., tr. and ed. *The Christological Controversy* (Melito through Chalcedon). Philadelphia, 1980.

Richard, Louis, *The Mystery of the Redemption*. Baltimore, 1965.

Rivière, Jean, *The Doctrine of the Atonement. A Historical Essay*. 2 vols., St. Louis, 1909.

Turner, H.E.W., *The Patristic Doctrine of the Redemption: A Study of the Development of Doctrine of the First Five Centuries*. London, 1952.

Vonier, Anscar, *The Victory of Christ*. New York, 1934.

Person, Author Index

Subject Index

Scriptural Index